Rational Sex Ethics

American University Studies

Series V
Philosophy

Vol. 73

PETER LANG
New York • Bern • Frankfurt am Main • Paris

Ben Neal Ard, Jr.

Rational Sex Ethics

Second Edition

PETER LANG
New York • Bern • Frankfurt am Main • Paris

Library of Congress Cataloging-in-Publication Data

Ard, Ben N.
   Rational sex ethics.
   2nd edition
   (American university studies. Series V, Philosophy ;
vol. 73)
   Bibliography: p.
   Includes index.
   1. Sexual ethics.   I. Title.   II. Series.
HQ32.A73   1989   306.7   88-8323
ISBN 0-8204-0857-3
ISSN 0739-6392

CIP-Titelaufnahme der Deutschen Bibliothek

Ard, Ben Neal:
Rational sex ethics / Ben Neal Ard, Jr. − 2. ed.
− New York; Bern; Frankfurt am Main; Paris:
Lang, 1989.
   (American University Studies: Ser. 5,
   Philosophy; Vol. 73)
   ISBN 0-8204-0857-3

NE: American University Studies / 05

Printed by Weihert-Druck GmbH, Darmstadt, West Germany

Dedicated, with respect and affection,
to the memory of my father:

Ben Neal Ard, M. D.
(1884-1938)

TABLE OF CONTENTS

ACKNOWLEDGEMENTS

When a book is published, it is customary to acknowledge the help the author received in writing the book. In this instance that is not an easy task since the book has been fermenting for many years and the author is indebted to many professors, clinicians, scholars, colleagues, students and friends with whom the ideas in the book have been discussed on many occasions.

While completing a Bachelor of Arts degree in psychology, with a minor in philosophy, at the University of California at Los Angeles, the author had the good fortune to study with Roy Dorcus and Knight Dunlap, among others. The author also had the privilege of studying scientific philosophy with Hans Reichenbach. Later, doing graduate study at the University of California at Berkeley, the author studied psychology with Harold E. Jones and Abraham Maslow, among others, and was a graduate research assistant at the Institute for Child Welfare.

The author learned much about human sex behavior while serving as a graduate assistant to Lester A. Kirkendall at Oregon State University at Corvallis, where he received a Master of Science degree in counseling, with a minor in psychology.

A year of clinical supervision was spent at the Merrill-Palmer Institute in Detroit where the author was a fellow in marriage counseling and family life education. He also had the intellectually stimulating experience of being supervised by and learning from Richard Kerckhoff, John Hudson, Clark Moustakas and others. He also came into contact with various visiting scholars there, among them Margaret Mead, Dorothy Lee, Ashley Montague, Lawrence K. Frank, Erich Fromm, William Masters and Virginia Johnson, among others.

At the University of Michigan in Ann Arbor, where he received an interdepartmental Ph.D. degree in education and psychology, he completed a dissertation on the sexual behavior and attitudes of marital partners married over twenty years. His major professor was E. Lowell Kelly (then chairman of the psychology department), and the members of his doctoral committee were Robert Blood, Allen Menlo and Richard Kerckhoff. While in Ann Arbor he also studied philosophy with Walter Kaufmann.

After completing his "formal" education, he had the good fortune to continue to learn from such scholars and clinicians as Albert Ellis, Robert A. Harper, Wardell Pomeroy, Ira Reiss, Nathaniel Branden, Clark Vincent and John Williams.

Having taught at several universities (Michigan State, the University of Michigan, Central Michigan University and San Francisco State University) the author has had discussions with colleagues and students at these institutions. Students have discussed many of these ideas in seminars (and sometimes extended post-seminars).

Finally, he would like to acknowledge the many clients who brought their problems to him in his private practice as a licensed psychologist and a licensed marriage, family and child counselor, as well as a certified sex therapist. They particularly are one of the main reasons for the writing of this book and have taught him much about the sex problems and the ethical dilemmas many people have in our culture. They have revealed their ubiquitous guilt and the many troublesome ethical dilemmas they have faced about sexual matters. Hopefully this book will help many others who may face similar situations in the future with less guilt and thus will be able to resolve their ethical dilemmas about sex in a more human, rational manner.

FORWARD

I am delighted with Ben Ard's <u>Rational Sex Ethics</u>, because it beautifully brings back into the field of sexual behavior an ethical, philosophic, and humanistic aspect that has largely been missing from most of the recent literature in the field. This was not true during the early part of the twentieth century, when Havelock Ellis started the ball rolling with a series of powerful books, especially his Studies in the Psychology of Sex, that not only presented a pioneering, objective and scientific attitude with a general ethical-humanistic framework.

Ellis's example was followed and augmented by many other early sexologists and social thinkers - including Walter Franklin Robie (<u>Rational Sex Ethics</u>, 1916, and <u>The Art of Love</u>, 1921), Ellen Key (<u>Love and Marriage</u>, 1911), Marie Stopes (<u>Married Love</u>, 1918), Harland William Long (<u>Sane-Sex Life and Sane-Sex Living</u>, 1919), William J. Robinson (<u>Treatment of Sexual Impotence</u>, 1915), and (<u>Woman: Her Sex and Love Life</u>, 1929). All these pioneers were primarily interested in teaching the public of their day the unadulterated facts of sex. But they also made sure that they put this material within an ethical framework; and they frankly espoused an attitude that was human rather than angelic, workable rather than purely idealistic, and firmly rooted in the realities of general and sexual behavior.

Ben Ard has courageously and incisively revived this liberal-humanistic tradition. Whereas most of the recent literature on sex has heavily presented research data and clinical material - witness, for example, the influential works of Alfred C. Kinsey and his associates, Masters and Johnson, Hartman and Faithian, Helen Kaplan, Joseph Lo Piccolo, Shere Hite and other who have followed in their footsteps - Dr. Ard's book builds on this kind of empirical research but also seriously questions and analyzes the general rules of ethics and makes a real effort to place sex ethics as a subheading under this more comprehensive perspective of human behavior. In doing so, he relevantly quotes many outstanding thinkers and scientists who have made sound contributions to ethical philosophy but whose works have often tended to be overlooked by recent come-latelies to the field of sex.

In the course of presenting his own view of rational sex ethics, Dr. Ard frequently quotes from my own writings, and shows that they significantly overlap with his ideas. In doing so, he fairly and accurately cites me; and he rightly implies that I would go along with almost all of his own notions. Reading his presentation has encouraged me to rethink some of my own views on sex and ethics and to summarize them briefly as follows:

Sex ethics and general ethics. A human act is virtually never good or bad because it is sexual or nonsexual. Sex ethics are merely a subheading under the more general rubric of human ethics. There are no absolute laws of morality, but humans in all cultures have a social contract to act in such a matter that they themselves are not unduly sabotaged or harmed by others and so that they, in turn, also do not unduly or needlessly sabotage or harm other humans in their society. Sex morals flow from general morals, and from this social contract; they virtually never exist in their own right.

The basis of ethics. Ethics, including sex ethics, are based on human wants and desires - on some form of hedonism. This has recently been well stated by Warren Shibles, in his book Ethics: A Critical Analysis for

Children (Whitewater, Wisconsin: The language Press, 1978), which can also
be read with great profit by virtually every adult:

> *Things are right or wrong because of what happens
> and what we want to happen. It is wrong for me to
> steal from you, because I do not want you or anyone
> else to steal from me. Also, I want you to be happy,
> and stealing from you would probably make you unhappy.
> Thus, it is wrong to steal because of what I want and
> what you want... A person steals when he does not
> understand what happens when he steal. Thus, to be
> ethical is to understand, to be intelligent. It is to know
> the results of our actions. To be ethical is also to
> understand our own wants and goals... The most ethical
> person is the one who is intelligent, knows himself and
> knows what happens because of his actions. To be
> ethical is merely to bring about your needs and wants
> effectively."*

Rational ethics and rational sex ethics. Rationality, in line with the
principles of rational-emotive therapy, mainly consists of choosing,
preferring, or wanting to act in a certain way - usually, so that this way
helps you to survive and be happy (that is, get more of what you want and
less of what you don't want) - and then aiding or abetting your own

choices and preferences. Irrationality mainly consists of choosing, preferring, or wanting to act in a certain way and then blocking or sabotaging your choices and preferences. Just as there are no absolute laws or rules of morality, so there are also no absolute or invariant laws of rationality. Warren Shibles states that to be ethical is merely to bring about your strong desires and wants effectively. In rational-emotive therapy (RET), I and my colleagues try to help people be rational (or rational-emotive) by bringing about their strong desires and wants effectively. We do not tell them what to desire or prefer; but show them how, once they choose their own desires or preferences, they can act logically and realistically to actualize their wishes. In the area of sexuality, we help them do the same thing: to help them choose sex goals, purposes, and ideals, and then to rationally, uncompulsively, and unabsolutistically - or, in a word, efficiently - try to achieve these goals.

Immorality and damnation. When people choose - as they often do - to act immorally or unethically, RET holds that they are never damnable or condemnable as humans. Their acts, deeds, performances, and traits may well be deemed "bad" or "irresponsible" - that is, needlessly sabotaging their own desires and/or those of other members of the social group with which they choose to live and relate - but they, the actors, are not bad people or rotten persons for performing these immoralities. Instead, they are invariably fallible, highly imperfect humans who have done and may still be doing wrong, stupid, or inefficient things. And their goal had better be to accept and forgive themselves while actively and determinedly trying to change their behaviors. RET teaches them - as Christianity theoretically is supposed to do but rarely does - to accept the sinner (themselves and other humans) while condemning, at most, his or her sinful or unethical acts. It also holds that, in sexual and nonsexual realms, condemning or damning people's "self," "being," "totality," "essence," or "personality" for their unethical deeds does more harm than good. For it encourages them to waste time and energy contemplating and rating their "egos" and deifying or devil-fying their "selves," instead of working like hell to modify their self-defeating and antisocial actions. Judging people rather than their doings helps them to get obsessed with proving instead of enjoying themselves.

This brief summary of my current ideas of general and sexual ethics significantly overlaps, as noted above, with most of the thinking expounded by Ben Ard in this book. In much more detail than I have just done, he outlines the humanistic basis for morality and then concretely applies it to some of our most important sexual problems. It is good to see such a vital area of life dealt with so thoughtfully and valuable. Dr. Ard wears many hats and competencies: as a scientist, a professor of psychology and counseling, a psychotherapist, a marriage and family counselor, a sexologist, and a humanistic philosopher. He brings all these proficiences to the writing of this book - for which its readers may well be thankful!

Albert Ellis, Ph.D.

Institute for Rational-Emotive Therapy

45 East 65th Street

New York, N. Y. 10021

"Today we are privileged not only to examine all of our traditions critically but to change our archaic beliefs; indeed, unless we deliberately close our eyes and ears and reject the new knowledge and the new understanding, we cannot avoid being critically aware of how much our traditional assumptions have become progressively incredible and inadequate, frequently misleading and defeating our efforts to live wisely."

Lawrence K. Frank
(1951, pp. 156-157)

PREFACE

This book is offered as an introduction to rational or humanistic sex ethics which are based on the latest scientific knowledge from pertinent disciplines. Recent advances in the field of sexology, psychology, anthropology, sociology and psychiatry need to be incorporated into a systematic reconsideration of sex ethics.

There is ample evidence that sexual practices can and do change. Studies such as those conducted by Kinsey and his associates (1948, 1953), Reiss (1960, 1967), and Hunt (1974), among others, clearly show some definite changes and significant trends, whether one labels what is happening as a "sexual revolution" or a "sexual renaissance."

What seems to be needed now is a reconsideration of the ethics of sexual acts and attitudes in the light of our growing knowledge, in order that those who wish to can make more rational choices of their goals in these matters, see the effect of there explicitly chosen ends, and recognize the results of using various means to achieve these purposes. This book will help in this regard.

This book does not approach sexual matters from the conventional or religious point of view. Thus it is not 'moralistic' in this sense. Those who wish a supernatural basis for their sex morality will have to look elsewhere. One of the main reasons for offering such a book as this lies in the rather obvious failure of the conventional religious morality to properly serve the function of a system of sex ethics.

Although this book includes the suggestion that we need to get rid of our conventional religious sex morality, it is still necessary to have some sex ethics. As Rene Guyon has ably pointed out,

> "the happiness or unhappiness of each of us -- often the happiness or unhappiness of whole peoples-- depends upon the manner in which we have conceived and directed our sexual lives, dealt with its various forms, and submitted its manifestations, voluntarily or involuntarily, to some social principle or philosophic system." (Guyon, 1948, p. 7)

The point of view set forth in this book is perhaps best called scientific humanism, although it probably would not be accepted in its entirety by any of the philosophers of the humanistic school (e.g., Morain & Morain, 1954; Otto, 1949; Rapoport, 1950, 1953). It follows wherever the facts lead and to that extent is empirical. The value judgments and assumptions underlying the book are explicitly stated in the chapter on basic principles and are closest, perhaps, to the philosophy of naturalistic or scientific humanism. For these reasons the term scientific humanism is used. The facts are open to anyone with a scientific or inquiring mind. The book is extensively documented in order that the interested reader may seek out the evidence for the various statements made. Essentially this book is an extension of the democratic ideal into the sexual sphere.

After a brief look at what is wrong with conventional sex morality, a chapter is devoted to the basic principles underlying the point of view advocated in this book, i.e., rational sex ethics. Then the principles are applied to various epochs in the life of the individual. Finally, various problems, or problem areas, are taken up and discussed in the light of these principles.

There have been other books which have pointed the way to a more rational sex ethics, some of them published many years ago, but none of the authors had the advantage of being able to base their conclusions on the most recent advances in our knowledge, such as the investigations by Kinsey and his associates (1948, 1953, Ford and Beach (1951), Reiss (1960, 1967), Masters and Johnson (1966, 1970, and Hunt (1974), to mention only a few.

The author has had a background of training and experience in psychology, marriage counseling and sex therapy, as well as sex education work with parents, elementary school pupils, high school students, and college students. The background of experience in marriage counseling and sex therapy and individual and group psychotherapy has been with people from all walks of life, from various parts of the United States, and some clients from other parts of the world. This background may be classified as that of the clinician working with individuals and groups.

Working in such circumstances, the author has been constantly faced with the impact of our conventional sex morality upon individual lives. And he has felt he had a further responsibility than that of merely helping the individual after that person has found himself or herself involved in psychological and sexual difficulties. As Wendell Johnson has pointed out, "the clinician, if he is to make his left hand support what his right hand is doing, has the responsibility of taking an active interest in those community and cultural changes that hold some degree of promise for bringing about more adequate conditions for human living." (Johnson, 1946, p. 425) This book is an attempt to fulfill part of this responsibility. The author feels an ethical responsibility to help the present and future generations adopt more rational attitudes toward human sexual behavior than previous generations have evidenced.

The book is not offered as the final word in these matters, since there can be no final word as long as further knowledge is forthcoming. It is merely offered as some tentative suggestions which seem warranted by our present state of knowledge. If it stimulates the thoughts of some readers along lines new to them, or encourages others to come forth with better suggestions along these lines, it has served a useful purpose.

Ben N. Ard, Jr., Ph. D.

San Francisco
1988

PREFACE REFERENCES

Ford, C. S. & Beach, F. A. Patterns of Sexual Behavior. New York: Harper, 1951.

Frank, Lawrence K. Nature and Human Nature. New Brunswick, N. J.: Rutgers University Press, 1951.

Guyon, Rene. The Ethics of Sexual Acts. New York: Knopf, 1948.

Hunt, Morton. Sexual Behavior in the 1970's. Chicago: Playboy Press, 1974.

Johnson, Wendell. People in Quandries. New York: Harper, 1946.

Kinsey, A. C., et al. Sexual Behavior in the Human Male. Philadelphia: Saunders, 1948.

Kinsey, A. C., et al. Sexual Behavior in the Human Female. Philadelphia: Saunders, 1953.

Masters, William H. & Johnson, Virginia E. Human Sexual Response. Boston: Little, Brown, 1966.

Masters, William H. & Johnson, Virginia E. Human Sexual Inadequacy. Boston: Little, Brown, 1970.

Morain, Lloyd & Morain, Mary. <u>Humanism as the Next Step</u>. Boston: Beacon Press, 1954.

Otto, Max C. <u>Science and The Moral Life</u>. New York: New American Library, 1949.

Rapoport, Anatol. <u>Science and the Goals of Man</u>. New York: Harper, 1950.

Rapoport, Anatol. <u>Operational Philosophy</u>. New York: Harper, 1953.

Reiss, Ira L. <u>Premarital Sexual Standards in America</u>. Glencoe: Free Press, 1960.

Reiss, Ira L. <u>The Social Context of Premarital Sexual Permissiveness</u>. New York: Holt, Rinehart & Winston, 1967.

"The religious codes have always and everywhere been the prime source of those social attitudes which, in their aggregate, represent the sexual mores of all groups, devout or non-devout, church going, rational, faithful to a creed, or merely following the custom of the land."

Kinsey, Pomeroy and Martin

(1948, p. 486)

CHAPTER 1
CONVENTIONAL SEX MORALITY

Introduction: The Problem of Sex in Our culture

Sex, and the ethical values involved in dealing with sex, present some of the most significant, pressing and unresolved problems facing people living in our culture today. While some people are able to deal reasonably well with their love, sex and marriage problems, many, if not most, people in our culture have difficulties in these areas of their lives. It may be seriously questioned, as one psychologist and marriage counselor, Dr. Albert Ellis, has put it,

> "whether most of our citizens get much sex-love-marriage satisfaction from living in our culture. It may more seriously be questioned whether most of them would not get considerably more such satisfaction if certain aspects of our culture, particularly our basic attitudes about sexual questions, were radically and rationally reorganized." (Ellis, 1954, p. 217)

It is the major thesis of this book that we had better work out a fundamental reconsideration of our conventional sex morality, and particularly along more rational, scientific and humanistic lines, if we are ever going to really resolve the sexual problems of our culture. However, as the sociologist Harry Elmer Barnes has stated,

> "Sexual activity is almost unique today in being regarded as a type of behavior which does not require explanation and control. It is still viewed by the majority of the members of society as the realm of conduct which is reserved for supernatural inspiration and guidance. As an influential contemporary churchman once put it, 'Little children come trooping down from Heaven.' Any attempt to introduce human wisdom into this realm, hitherto monopolized by supernaturalism, is viewed as both wicked and presumptuous. It is held that a general air of mystery should prevail here. A minimum of such knowledge as we require should be sought in revealed scriptures and theological dogmas." (Barnes, 1939, p. 382)

This attitude toward all serious discussion of sexual questions poses difficult problems to anyone suggesting that there are other (and better) ways of looking at these matters than the traditional or conventional way. The social historian Harry Elmer Barnes has thrown light on this problem too. He has said

> "The thesis that there is but one right and divinely revealed way of dealing with sexual or any other human situations is dealt a deathblow by the recognition that there have been literally hundreds of different methods whereby man has handled every social issue and

situation, and that in each case he has regarded his
solution as perfect and the product of divine inspiration."
(Barnes, 1939, p. 416)

It goes without saying that the present author holds no brief for any conclusions reached in this book as being either perfect or of divine inspiration. Rather, they are an attempt to re-evaluate the sexual problems of our time and culture through the use of the best thinking of scientists from the various pertinent disciplines. Following the scientific credo, then, any conclusions reached are always seen in the light of present knowledge and subject to revision as newer knowledge is gained.

* * *

Counseling or psychotherapy is frequently needed for most individuals who have serious problems in the sexual area and is probably the ultimate way to their changing their attitudes toward sexual matters. However, while problems in the sexual area arise in individuals, it seems, because of particular experiences, even psychotherapists (at least some) realize that many, if not most, of the sexual problems in our culture derive from social factors.

Too often, many people (including even some psychotherapists) take the sexual mores as "given" and then see the sexual problem as merely the individual's idiosyncratic reaction to that problem. One psychotherapist, however, has clearly stated our point here:

"At bottom, the sabotaging of human sex-love
relations is a problem which is socially rather than
individually created, and which therefore cannot be solved
on a broad scale without widespread societal changes in

sex attitudes." (Ellis, 1954, pp. 264-265)
Corroborating weight is added by the psychiatrist Clara Thompson who has noted that"Sex is not the same kind of problem in a culture which does not inhibit it or degrade it as it is a problem in our society." (Thompson, 1950, p. 142)

* * *

In a book suggesting a fundamental reconsideration of sex ethics a basic question would seem to be: what is wrong with the sexual morality we already have? Some people feel that there would be no problems in this area if everyone would just follow the "accepted" code. However, it is one of the major arguments of this book that problems would not cease in this area of human relations even if everyone would follow the conventional codes more strictly. In fact, the situation would probably become worse if everyone followed the conventional sex morality to the letter. This book in its entirety may be seen to validate that statement.

Too many of the recent books which have dealt with sex and the problems related to it in our culture have considered "solutions" which were primarily "reformulations" of the same age-old approach tried and found wanting in the past. In these ways of writing too many authors seem afraid of any thoroughgoing attack on this problem of sex ethics versus conventional sexual morality (largely religious) since any such discussion must, of necessity, be controversial. As Philip Wylie has said of one recent book (The Decline and Fall of Sex, by the theologian Robert Elliot Fitch), "his solution of a problem (which Freud and other scientists, along with writers and theologians agree to be real) is Cotton Mather's solution, Anthony Comstock's, Jonathan Edward's and John S. Sumner's. Viz:

We must return to the 'single standard' and to that socio-ecclesiastical brain-washing which induces guilt and nastiness-of-self in all who transgress the narrowest possible bounds of 'virtue.' Puritanism, in effect, alone can restore love to sex relations, Fitch avers.

Yet medicine, sociology, anthropology, and psychology (including Freud's) have made it indisputably clear that our national nastiness was partly caused and is much increased by the very 'morality' to which the Reverend Fitch would have us regress. Virginity maintained by built-in fear, fidelity induced by guilt, chastity invoked by sex-contamination, do not lead, in any enlightened group, to virtue or to love. Ask the doctors and asylum-keepers." Wylie, 1957, p. 25)

Thus the crux of any thoroughgoing solution of the sexual problems of our culture must be the realization that much of the difficulties in this area are the result of the conventional sex morality.

A. The Assumptions and Expectations of the Conventional Code

But what is the conventional sex code? Is there a conventional sex code? In one sense, of course, there is not one conventional sex code but many in our culture. There are different items in the sex codes followed in the various socio-economic classes (lower, middle, upper), for example, although the two extremes seem to be converging upon the middle class as a dominant code. Ethnic and racial sub-cultures have different views regarding acceptable racial behavior. Specific religious groups, slum groups and particular occupational groups have different codes. (Cavan, 1953, pp. 323-325)

In what sense, then, can we say that there is a code of acceptable (and unacceptable) sexual behavior and attitudes which might justifiably be called conventional sex morality? In this book we shall use the phrase conventional sex morality to mean the dominant, "ideal," most influential and widely accepted code in our culture as a whole. Specifically, too, this code is that advocated by conventional people (i. e.l, "good," "respectable" people) as well as the "moral leaders" of our society.

Another difficulty arises immediately, namely that nowhere in print (as far as the author knows) is there a specific, detailed inventory of conventional sex morality which would be completely acceptable to everyone concerned. For example, let us consider the very general and brief statement by Harry Elmer Barnes:

> *"Our sex mores and family institutions embody: (1) primitive reaction to the mystery of sex and of women in particular; (2) Hebraic uxoriousness and conception of patriarchal male domination; (3) patristic and medieval views regarding the baseness of sex and of sex temptation, especially as offered by women; (4) the medieval esteem for virginity in women; (5) the sacramental view of marriage, which leads us to regard marriage as a theological rather than a social issue; (6) the property views of the early bourgeoisie; and (7) the Kantian rationalization of personal inadequacy and inexperience. There is not a single item in the sex mores of a conventionally respectable American today which squares with either science or aesthetics." (Barnes, 1929, p. 19)*

Now this very general and brief inventory of conventional sex morality would probably be cause for considerable argument among many people in our culture and particularly the so-called moral leaders. Each item would probably arouse a negative reaction in someone. And we have not really spelled out in much detail an inventory which includes specific values and attitudes on the wide variety of sexual problems in our culture. This is the difficulty inherent in any "inventory" on such a controversial subject.

If one reads the apologists for conventional sex morality, there is little likelihood of encountering many disagreeable or harmful items, or very many fundamental criticisms of conventional sex morality. Many if not most of the more harmful conventional sexual attitudes are rarely admitted explicitly by so-called "modern" moral leaders or the "modern" people who accept them and live by them. As the psychologist Albert Ellis has put it,

> "At least half our possible sex and marriage views, in other words, are never allowed into consciousness for rational examination. Psychologically speaking, we do not merely suppress such views: we thoroughly repress them. We deny that we could have ever possibly thought of them, and refuse to face the fact of their potential existence." (Ellis, 1954, p. 221)

In this book, however, we shall hear from the real critics of conventional sex morality so as to get at the basic faults and weaknesses of the conventional codes. We do not need alibis at this point, merely the truth, unpleasant and unpopular though it may be. Many of the statements and conclusions in this book may seem provocative, controversial and hard to take for the person who has followed the traditional, conventional code (and some even to those of a more liberal bent). But if they stimulate critical thinking about sex ethics they will have served a useful purpose.

Let us consider, then, some of the basic assumptions and expectations of conventional sex morality. (It will not be feasible to consider every conceivable dicta regarding sexual behavior, such as the Roman Catholic writers were wont to do in medieval times.) In the following "inventory" of some of the basic ideas which make up conventional sex morality in our culture it is obvious that different individuals hold such views in varying degrees. Some non-conventional individuals hold none of the views mentioned, while other, more conventional individuals, would hold perhaps all of them. Most conventional people would hold something like many of these views, although each individual would naturally phrase the particular beliefs somewhat differently (in so far as he or she is even aware that their actions imply such views). Here we have tried to state the essence of these basic ideas in their simplest, clearest fashion. The order in which the ideas are presented follows roughly the order in which they will be discussed in this and the following chapters. No other assumptions regarding the relative importance of the various ideas is intended by the particular order of presentation. Throughout the later chapters we shall consider in greater detail the conventional views on sexual matters, here we shall merely take an overview of conventional sex morality and what is wrong with these views, rather than an exhaustive description.

Conventional sex morality, then, includes the ideas that:

1. All forms of sexual behavior are by nature suspect, and only those that make up a bare minimum essential for the purpose of reproduction, are permissible.

2. Sex is illegitimate unless it is limited (ideally) to one person

throughout life (i. e., lifelong monogamy for both persons) and even then exercised only in certain approved ways within marriage.

3. Every individual can easily adjust himself or herself to the same pattern of sexual activity (i. e., the conventional ideal).

4. All manifestations of the sexual impulse are the essence of evil. (That is, sexual pleasure is sinful.)

5. The essence of the "original sin" in the Garden of Eden was the concupiscence which accompanied the act of generation. Sex is thus the worst sin since it was the first sin and led to the downfall of humankind and therefore all of their subsequent difficulties.

6. Women should be subservient to men in sexual matters and children subservient to adults. Anyone who goes against the conventional sex code should be subservient to conventional people and be harshly dealt with by the powers that be, as an example and warning to others.

7. Anyone's private sex life (even in marriage) is subject to control, supervision, interference and censorship by neighbors, preachers, judges, policeman, and any "good" (i. e., conventional) person.

8. Many sexual acts are forbidden, even when they occur between two willing, mature adults (even when married to each other), and no harmful consequences result.

9. Children conceived "out of wedlock" (i. e., before marriage) are "illegitimate" and thus do not deserve to be treated as other children are.

10. Sexual strivings in children are "bad" (including just about any manifestation of sex, and even some actually non-sexual manifestations which adults interpret as sexual).

11. There is no clearly approved outlet for natural sex drives until

marriage, no matter how late. (This precludes any premarital intercourse.)

12. Birth control (or planned parenthood) is "wrong" since it interferes with "God's plan" for sex: reproduction.

13. Sex in marriage must be confined to certain "approved" techniques and methods, and only those techniques and methods.

14. All extra-marital sex is wrong.

15. Interracial marriages are forbidden.

16. Interfaith marriages should be discouraged.

17. Divorce is not approved since lifelong monogamy is the ideal.

18. No sex life for the unmarried adult is permissible.

19. Homosexuality should be harshly dealt with in any suspected form since it is against "God's law."

20. The sexual offender (including anyone who breaks any aspect of the conventional sex code) should be severely punished in any case as an example and warning to others and for the salvation of his own soul.

Immediately upon reading such ideas (at least some of them), many people will probably say that these ideas are not a part of conventional sex morality. This is one of the difficulties in listing any such inventory; too often an argument ensues immediately as to whether these ideas are really a part of conventional sex morality. Do very many people in our culture believe such ideas or act in such a way as to demonstrate they are following such ideas implicitly? This chapter, and the remaining chapters of the book, will include evidence that a great many people in our culture do still in fact (implicitly, if not explicitly) believe in and act upon such ideas.

B. The Origins and Development of the Conventional Code

The next question which may occur to the perceptive reader is: where do such ideas ultimately come from? The average person, when asked what is behind conventional sex morality might say "social pressures." However, that these social pressures are primarily religious in their origins is confirmed by the studies of Kinsey and his associates. (Kinsey, et al, 1948, p. 468) Although no social level accepts the whole of the original Judeo-Christian code, each level derives its taboos from some part of the same religious outlook. (Kinsey, et al, 1948. p. 487) Despite significant differences on many theological points among different religious denominations, there are only minor differences in the emphasis which the several religious groups have placed upon sex morality. (Kinsey, et al, 1948, p. 483)

There is, however, considerable discrepancy between the professed religious codes and the actual patterns of sexual behavior found in our culture, as Kinsey, et al (1953) have demonstrated.

> "These apparent conflicts between the religious codes and the patterns of sexual behavior may lead one to overlook the religious origins of the social patterns. Nevertheless, the individual who denies that he is in any way influenced by church rulings still stoutly defends the church's system of natural law, recognizes certain behavior as unnatural, abnormal, and perverse, or considers that certain things (but only certain things) are fine, aesthetically satisfactory, socially expedient, and decent for a mature and intelligent male to engage in. In so contending, he perpetuates the tradition of the Judaic law and the Christian precept." (Kinsey, et al, 1948, p. 487)

Today "the influence of the church is more indirect; but the ancient religious codes are still the prime sources of the attitudes, the ideas, the ideals, and the rationalizations by which most individuals pattern their sexual lives." (Kinsey, et al, 1948, p. 487)

Kinsey and his associates have pointed out that,

> *"the ancient codes have been accepted by laymen, jurists, and scientists alike as the ultimate sources of moral evaluations, of present-day legal procedure, and of the list of subjects that may go into a textbook of abnormal psychology. In no other field of science have scientists been satisfied to accept the biologic notions of ancient jurists and theologians, or the analyses made by the mystics of two or three thousand years ago." (Kinsey, et al, 1948, p. 203)*

Thus the simplest and most direct answer to the question about where our conventional sex morality comes from is that it is derived, ultimately, from the Judeo-Christian view of sex. But here again we are faced with the question: what is "the Judeo-Christian view of sex"?

Writing about "the Judeo-Christian view of sex" is, in one sense, an almost impossible task. For one thing, throughout Judeo-Christian history there have been many different points of view expressed about sex, all claiming to be "Christian." Deciding which views properly represent "true Christianity" is one task that all those who call themselves Christians would probably never agree upon. For example, when contemporary Christians run across an idea or statement about sex which they disagree with (possibly because it does not jibe with modern scientific thinking) they frequently then refuse to believe what the author of the statement wrote, or they pretend that the author wrote something quite different than what he actually did, or they at least insist that he "really meant" something entirely different. Thus it is increasingly difficult to formulate a statement of what the Christian view of sex is which would be completely acceptable to all.

However, perhaps we can describe the "main stream" of Christian thinking on sex. The plural marriages of Mormons, for example, or the views accepted in the Oneida community experiment, or the extremely liberal views of some "modern" theologians, then, are not a part of the main stream of Christian thinking about sex (no matter what their originators may claim). On the other hands, the views of men like Paul, Augustine, Luther, Calvin and later Puritans and writers of the Victorian age are definitely a part of the main stream of Christian thought, certainly as Christian sex morality has grown and been generally accepted and understood by most people today.

Some readers may question the value or necessity of tracing the conventional sexual views back to their historical origins. Why bother with such "ancient history"? The social historian Harry Elmer Barnes has provided us with an answer:

> "It may be predicted that most of our ignorant and senseless prejudices on sex matters would be removed in a generation or so if the intellectual leaders in society could profit by systematic and accurate instruction in the historical development of our contemporary sex practices and ideas." (Barnes, 1939, p.417)

In the Bible itself there are different and contradictory views of sex. This gets into the old question of which "parts" of the Bible are to be accepted, or is every word to be accepted literally? Unfortunately, as Mangasarian has pointed out, "Religion has so perverted the judgement of men that they admire in the Bible what they would despise anywhere else." (Mangasarian, 1911, p.147)

Nevertheless, there is some consistency or agreement in the main lines of Christian thought about sex, even from parts of the Old Testament down to present-day theologians' writings. For example, as the modern Protestant theologian Seward Hiltner has pointed out,

> *"In those parts of the Old Testament that reflect the historically earliest conceptions of the Hebrew people, we find a conception of sex like that of the 'mana' of which the anthropologists speak a kind of mysterious, external, and wholly supernatural force that invades human life and human beings for good or for ill." (Hiltner, 1943, p. 8)*

Then, if we read present-day theologians such as W. Norman Pittinger (1954), or Roland H. Bainton (1957), for example, we still find this strong supernatural, mysterious element underlying their view of Christian sex morality today.

It would take at least another large volume to delineate the detailed origins of the present-day religious codes which apply to sex, and to trace the subtle ways in which these codes have influenced the behavior of individuals today. It is sufficient here to point out that our particular systems of sex codes are quite ancient and that they are the product of still older religious systems. (Kinsey, et al, 1948, p.465). And, as Geoffrey May has stated in his book Social Control of Sex Expression, "The Christian attitude had grown out of the Hebrew attitude, which in turn had been an adaptation of the practices of many primitive people as to the rights of property and the reactions of superstition." (May, 1931, p. 54)

The Judeo-Christian religion is based fundamentally on the basic supposition, which is assumed without question, that there exists somewhere a "heaven," a life after death which is both better and more permanent than this life on earth. But the convert, in order to insure his admission to this supposedly heavenly hereafter, is told that he must renounce the pleasures of this life on earth. In this way, sex, as one of the most insistent, perennial and intense of human pleasures, is circumscribed with innumerable prohibitions. (Guyon, 1948, p. 129)

The English physician and physiologist Alex Comfort, in his book Sexual Behavior in Society, has stated that

"The net impact of Christian teaching over nineteen centuries upon the public mind in our own culture has produced several clear-cut assumptions: that of all moral delinquencies, sexual misdeeds are the most serious; that sexuality in itself is a trap fraught with ritual and personal danger; that suffering, abstinence, and virginity are desirable as indices of moral value; and that right sexual conduct on the ethical plane is identical with the most suppressive mores of the group, not only in social matters, such as marital fidelity, but in details of custom, such as the avoidance of nakedness." (Comfort, 1950, p.66)

If the conclusions just stated by Comfort seem too hard on Christianity, perhaps because they come from a liberal point of view, let us turn to the

16

eminently respectable Reinhold Niebuhr, one of the most influential of contemporary Protestant theologians.

> *"he admits that the revolt of secular romanticism and naturalism against the sexual negativism of the Church, both Catholic and Protestant, is justified. Neither segment of Christianity has successfully related sexual life either to the total personality or to the total society. Catholicism's emphasis upon procreation must bear equal responsibility with Protestant Puritanism for the difficulties modern man encounters in his efforts to relate his sexual drives creatively to the whole of his life."* (Cole, 1955, pp. 188-189)

Another defender of the Christian view of sex, the English writer John Langdon-Davies, has said that

> *"the main thesis of Christian sexual morality stands out clear for all to read. No sexual act was legitimate save for the natural purpose of creating children within holy matrimony, except in those cases when the sexual act could take place without possibility of procreation because of some natural transient obstacle. Thus intercourse during pregnancy was not prohibited although procreation was then out of the question, since the natural law was not being wilfully disobeyed." (Langdon-Davies, 1954, p.75)*

And, as Langdon-Davies added, "it is certain that Christianity alone among religions set itself such an extreme purpose." (Langdon-Davies, 1954, p. 75)

One of the central tenets of the Judeo-Christian religion is the concept of sin. This theological supposition started out as a violation of the so-called will of God. Out of this general concept there arose the specific doctrine of "original sin." This was a curse which the Judeo-Christian God was supposed to have inflicted upon all subsequent generations of humans because of the transgression of the so-called first man, Adam, and his wife, Eve. The Christian religion has fostered this "sense of sin" with its accompanying feelings of inadequacy, unworthiness and guilt. And, as the sociologist Harry Elmer Barnes has pointed out,

> "The notion of sin is probably the most potent weapon in the whole armory of orthodoxy. Without it there would be little rationale in the whole Christian scheme of things. ... Once we wipe out the validity of the notion of sin there would appear to be slight justification for the ministrations and activities of the church." (Barnes, 1929, pp. 208-209)

The Christian apologist usually tries to maintain that this "sense of sin," or in modern terminology, guilt, is an inherent part of man's nature rather than admitting that it is engendered by the teachings of religion. One psychiatrist, Abram Kardiner, in his book Sex and Morality, has pointed out the need to think differently on this matter: "Guilt is not an inborn emotion like fear or rage. It is a cultivated emotion. We cannot, therefore, assume its existence in a perpetual state and its perpetuation as a part of man's inherited equipment." (Kardiner, 1954, p. 118) Later in this chapter we shall hear from the psychologist Erich Fromm about how this guilt is tied to sex.

The legitimacy of sex as seen by Christianity has been clearly spelled out by one of the defenders of the Christian view, John Langdon-Davies, in his book Sex, Sin and Sanctity (1954). Extracting the main definition of a legitimate sex act, he has written thusly:

> "A sexual act is only moral between a married couple; its object must be procreation, unless a natural impediment such as pregnancy or involuntary sterility persists; it must be performed in a manner apt to procreation and the slightest deviation in position which might be construed as contraceptive in purpose or in effect is sin. Moreover a study of the innumerable textbooks of moral theology shows that married couples are in danger of falling into error if the degree of pleasure exceeds that which is absolutely necessary for the procreative act." (Langdon-Davies, 1954, pp. 82-83)

Homer W. Smith, in his definitive book Man and His Gods, has concluded that

> "Christianity undermined the family, the unit of the social system, by teaching that celibacy is an exalted virtue; and by its emphasis on continence it directed the sexual impulse into physical and psychological perversions. It dogmatically relegated women to an inferior position, socially, politically and intellectually, and by making a sacrament of marriage it permitted wives to become chattels and husbands boors. It supplanted courage and initiative by resignation: Providence had arranged things in their order, the rich and the poor, the well and

*the sick, the wise and the ignorant; and to question
Providence was to question the wisdom of God. Misery
was to be tolerated patiently in anticipation of
everlasting glory. It did not highly esteem either personal
or political freedom, and in no case was it prepared to
fight for them." (Smith, 1952, p. 228)*

Commenting further about Christianity, Homer Smith wrote,

*"For the sense of the dignity of man, fundamental to
the precepts of the Stoicks and of Cicero, Seneca, Marcus
Aurelius and other Roman moralists, it substituted the
doctrine of personal inadequacy, the sense of guilt, and
the habits of self-doubt and self-abnegation. In its
cardinal doctrine...it promulgated a belief which was to
crucify the whole of the western world for centuries to
come." (Smith, 1952, p. 229)*

If this analysis seems too hard on Christianity, let us turn to a Professor
of pastoral Theology and Christian Social Ethics at the Episcopal Theological
School, Joseph Fletcher, who has written these words:

*"First of all it needs saying that the Christian
churches must shoulder much of the blame for the
confusion, ignorance, and unhealthy guilt associations
which surround sex in Western culture...sex for its own
sake was always scorned. ...there have been, beginning in
the primitive church, many puritanical Christians, both
Catholic and Protestant, who have treated sexuality as
something inherently evil." (Fletcher, quoted in Doniger,*

1953, p. 188)

Robert Briffault, an anthropologist, has pointed out that among the early Jews the conception of ritual defilement became modified with them into that of moral impurity or sin. "Out of that identification arose the ascetic ideals which characterized early Christianity, and in particular the fierce denunciation of all manifestations of the sexual instinct as the essence of evil." (Briffault, in Calverton & Schmalhausen, 1929, p. 49) In addition,

> *"The uncompromising attitude of the Christian Fathers, which caused many Christian converts to castrate themselves, condemned marriage as inconsistant with religion, pronounced women to be the gate of hell, and declared the extinction of the human race to be preferable to its propagation through sexual intercourse, has afforded the foundation of those standards of sexual morality which has ever since been current in the tradition of Western civilization." (Briffault, in Calverton & Schmalhausen, 1929, p.49)*

* * *

Some people may feel that, while the criticisms mentioned above apply to the Christian view of sex in its early history, "modern" Christians rely more on the views of Jesus and the New Testament rather than the older views. What about this objection? To answer it we turn to the contemporary Protestant theologian Joseph Fletcher who has pointed out that

> *"The New Testament is strikingly fragmentary in its treatment of sex problems and ethics. Jesus, for example, had nothing whatever to say about courtship, perversions,*

masturbation, sex manners, codes of reproduction and parenthood, multiple marriage, incest, birth control, artificial insemination, foeticide, and the like. Apart from his divorce teaching Jesus spoke only of the subjective side of sex. ... Modern depth psychology reveals so much about the unconscious and involuntary causes of our thoughts that some feel Jesus' ethical subjectivity was unjust." (Fletcher, in Doniger, 1953, p. 187)

Since Jesus did not comment upon any of the sexual problems mentioned above, and he said he did not come to change any of the old laws, we are forced to assume that he agreed with the views prevalent at that time as expressed by the moral leaders then.

Actually Jesus' rather sketchy views on sex were over-shadowed by later leaders of the church. As the social historian Harry Elmer Barnes has noted, "The most influential personage in the apostolic age was Paul, who did more to shape the early Christian attitude toward sex than did Christ and all the other apostles combined. His attitude was a combination of asceticism and morbidity." (Barnes, 1939, p. 385) St. Paul advised against marriage and parenthood except in cases of urgent sexual appetite. (I Corinthians 7)

Writing about early Christian views of sex, the theologian Joseph Fletcher has said, "St. Jerome could only praise marriage (the only permissible sexual partnership) because it produced virgins! St. Augustine went so far as to argue that coitus is sinful within wedlock unless the specific purpose is always conception." (Fletcher, in Doniger, 1953, p. 189) But even before its ascetic period Christianity had taught the evil of sex, as Geoffrey May has noted. (May, 1931, pp. 45-45)

"The religious reason for the ascetic's hatred of sex was the association of sex with the fall of man. The sin in the Garden of Eden, St. Augustine maintained, had caused the sex organs to become the seat of lust. In Paradise the act of generation would have been free from sexual desire and free from shame. These members would have been as pure as other parts of the body. But the original sin was hereditary; because of Adam sexual expression remained an evil." (May, 1931, p. 46)

"The ascetic christians translated into church doctrine their condemnation of the sexual impulse. They made all forms of extra-marital sex expressions sin, and all action even vaguely conducive to it. Because they thought virginity the prime virtue, they looked askance at marriage, and succeeded in enacting canons against the marriage of a widow..." (May, 1931, pp. 46-47)

To dissuade those who feel that such views no longer apply today, Pope Pius XII, in 1957, still urged widows not to remarry. (TIME, Sept. 30, 1957, p. 60)

"Because sexual activity was a complete evil, the absence of sexual activity came to be thought a complete good," as Geoffrey May put it. (May, 1931, p. 47)

"With the exception of a lifelong union of one man with one woman, the early Church pronounced as mortal sins all forms of sexual relations. Those not united in wedlock were forbidden by the Church so much as to kiss each other. Any sexual desire in the unmarried, even

thought unaccompanied by an external act, was regarded as sinful." (May, 1931, p. 47)

Paul Blanshard has stated that "In the Augustinian conception the sexual act was sinful in itself, and the essence of the original sin in the Garden of Eden was the concupiscence which accompanied the act of generation." (Blanshard, 1949, p. 135) Turning to Roland H. Bainton, Professor of Ecclesiastical Church History at the Yale University Divinity School, we find that he has said that 'Augustine brought to formulation the mature view of the early church with regard to sexual relations and marriage.'" (Bainton, in Doniger, 1953, p. 39) According to Bainton, Augustine felt that 'If we could have children in any other way we would refrain entirely from sex. Since we cannot, we indulge regretfully. Augustine almost voices the wish that the Creator had contrived some other device.' (Bainton, in Doniger, 1953, p. 41) Augustine felt that, with regard to sex, 'Procreation is the end and is not impeded in any other way than through continence.'" (Bainton, in Doniger, 1953, p. 42)

Continuing his analysis of Christian views regarding sex, Bainton has said that "During the early church and Middle Ages the prevailing view of sex was disparaging. Marriage was sacramental, lifelong, primarily for progeny, unromantic, and rating below virginity." (Bainton, in Doniger, 1953, p. 50) "Virginity was constantly exalted as an ideal. And at the same time those committed to celibacy strengthened their own resolve by berating the female sex. And anti-feminist literature became rife." (Bainton, in Doniger, 1953, p. 49)

In view of the evidence already seen so far we could concur with Alex Comfort that it seems undeniable that in sexual morals and practice

Christianity's influence has been less healthy than that of other world religions. It created a system of sexual morality and a resulting attitude toward sexuality at once rigid, antagonistic to the observable facts of human character and behavior, and based primarily upon fear, all in the framework of the supposed imminent end of the world. (Comfort, 1950, p. 63)

* * *

The Christian apologist might say that all of the foregoing may be true but the Protestant Reformation changed all that, at least for the Protestants. What about this objection?

In as much as our society may be described as predominantly a Protestant culture, how has this affected conventional sex morality? The view of man held by Luther and Calvin has been of tremendous influence on the development of modern Western society. As Erich Fromm has said, "they laid down the foundations for an attitude in which man's own happiness was not considered to be the aim of life but where he became a means, an adjunct, to ends beyond him, of an all-powerful God ..." (Fromm, 1947, p. 121)

> *"Calvin and Luther had taught that man must suppress his self-interest and consider himself only an instrument for God's purposes. Progressive thinkers, on the contrary, have taught that man ought to be only an end for himself and not a means for any purposes transcending him." (Fromm, 1947, pp. 135-135)*

Erich Fromm himself, a psychoanalyst and social psychologist, has illustrated just such progressive thinking in his book Man for Himself (1947).

The rise of Puritanism and the Mid-Victorian period, which followed from the teachings of the Protestant Reformation, can hardly be considered as much of an improvement in sex morality from earlier Christian beliefs. As Alex Comfort has pointed out, the tendency of much of even more recent Protestant moral teaching has been to reassert in terms of "social science" the same standards it formerly taught in terms of revelation; the general position of the Roman Catholic Church is fundamentally unchanged in sexual matters since the Middle Ages. (Comfort, 1950, pp. 66-67) All in all, "the traditional view of Christian civilizations has been that all forms of sexual behavior are by nature suspect, and that only those that make up a bare minimum, essential for the purposes of reproduction, are permissible." (Comfort, 1950, p. 16)

If Alex Comfort's views are felt to be too hard on Christianity, let us turn to a defender of the Christian view, John Langdon-Davies, who has said,

> "Western Europe dominated the world because, among other reasons, the Christian religion reduced the sexual activities, in theory and to a great extent in practice, to the bare minimum needed for the propagation of the species. There is no other part of the world where the dominant religion lays down that sexual intercourse is legitimate only within marriage and for the production of children..." (Langdon-Davies, 1954, p. 21)

Max Lerner, in his book America as a Civilization, has said, "Looking backward, one sees that the more rigid Puritan tradition stressed the Biblical virtues which limited sex to procreation and then led to widespread repression, hypocrisy, frustrations, and neuroses." (Lerner, 1957, p. 687) A formidable indictment, indeed.

The sociologist Ruth Cavan has stated that

> *"Puritanism identified sex with the baser qualities of
> human nature. ... the Puritan leaders sought to confine
> sex within the boundaries of family life, where its chief
> function was defined in terms of reproduction. Sex outside
> marriage was sinful, and heavy penalties were applied not
> only to actual sexual misconduct but to such behavior as
> kissing in public... the Puritan attitude toward sex as
> sinful is still accepted in some religious groups and is
> widely influential in the attitude toward non-marital sex
> behavior." (Cavan, 1953, p. 374)*

The reader who is interested in following the details of the cross-currents of ideas about sex from colonial times to the present day in America may turn with profit to Sidney Ditzion's book, Marriage, Morals and Sex in America: A History of Ideas (1953).

* * *

The sociologist Ruth Cavan, in her book The American Family, has analyzed changing views on sex in a chapter on "Sexual Behavior." (Cavan, 1953, pp. 367-396) Among the many conclusions she reached pertinent to our discussion are the following:

> *"During the nineteenth century the moral standard
> was complete virginity of both man and woman at the
> time of marriage, combined with complete fidelity be
> tween the two as long as both were alive. In the few*

instances where a divorce occurred, the social expectation
was that there would be no remarriage. Lifelong
monogamy one man with one woman was the ideal."
(Cavan, 1953, p. 381)

Cavan discussed the kinds of norms societies have imposed and adopted Ford and Beach's classification of societies into restrictive, semi-restrictive and permissive. She agreed with Ford and Beach when she concluded: "The United States in the past was legally and religiously a restrictive society." (Cavan, 1953, p. 372) She presented some data to support her view that the United States has been moving toward a semi-restrictive society. (Cavan, 1953, pp. 372ff) According to Cavan, the 1920's ushered in changing sexual behavior, but she also pointed out that "The reaction of community leaders and other adults was one of shock and protest." (Cavan, 1953, pp. 378-379) "Also, regardless of the deviations and violations that always existed, a fairly united front was presented by adults, leaders and laymen alike, on the meaning of sex and the relation of sex behavior to social welfare." (Cavan, 1953, p. 374) And Cavan has also pointed out that "Public disapproval dictates secrecy for emerging ways that contradict the traditional codes." (Cavan, 1953, p. 39)

Finally, in her analysis Cavan noted a recent rend back toward the restrictive society in that there have been many attempts to "reinterpret" the old restrictions in the light of "reason" which would be more "acceptable" to moderns. As Cavan put it, "Complete acceptance of this point of view would return the United States to the status of a restrictive society, but with new values supporting the restrictions." (Cavan, 1953, pp. 383-384) As an example of thus using "new values" to support old restrictions, Cavan has herself provided a prize specimen when she wrote: "...premarital sex relations are conducive to stunted personality development..." (Cavan, 1953, p. 385)

Turning to another analysis of American sexual expression, Max Lerner in his book <u>America as a Civilization</u>, has devoted a section to "Society and Sexual Expression." (Lerner, 1957, pp. 677-688) Among the many pertinent observations Lerner made re the following:

> *"Every society imposes regulations and codes upon sexual relations, but the striking fact here is that American codes, permissive in most other areas of behavior, are more restrictive about sex. ...sex is locked in an anomalous position within the frame of American society. The American cannot help becoming aware of the gap between what the society formally exacts of him in this area and what it allows him in almost every other. From the start sex is separated from the rest of life, surrounded with stronger (and therefore more exciting) prohibitions, banned except within the traditional forms and inside the limits of marriage." (Lerner, 1957, pp. 677-678)*

Some have felt that after World War I there was more evading of the sexual code.

> *"But there has been little relaxation of tensions. The figures on mental health suggest that the psychic strains of American life were at least as heavy in the mid-1950's as they were before World War I. What happened is that*

the forms and sources of the strain changed. Sexual life in America grew freer in breaking and evading the taboos, but conscience in the face of the codes remained, and as long as it did the evasion of the taboos remained a source of anxiety and guilt." (Lerner, 1957, p. 678)

Lerner has suggested that "Despite crosscurrents and counter-remedies the full sweep of the broad stream of the American sexual revolution has scarcely yet been felt." (Lerner, 1957, p. 683) And also,

> *"despite the fluid nature of American society there is a tenacity in the codes that is hard to break through, and their hold is all the greater because the loose and sprawling character of the society frightens most Americans and makes them cling all the harder to the challenged codes." (Lerner, 1957, p. 686)*

C. Some of the Effects of Conventional Sex Morality

After tracing in brief fashion some of the origins and later development of conventional sex morality we now turn to what effects the expectations of the conventional code have upon individuals living under it. As we shall see, it has not been easy.

One of the fundamental assumptions of conventional sex morality, which is completely erroneous, is the expectation that every individual can easily adjust himself or herself to the same pattern of sexual activity (i.e., the conventional ideal). As Kinsey and his associates have put it,

> *"The publicly pretended code of morals, our social organization, our marriage customs, our sex laws, and our*

> *educational and religious systems are based upon an*
> *assumption that individuals are much alike sexually, and*
> *that it is an equally simple matter for all of them to*
> *confine their behavior to the single pattern which the*
> *mores dictate." (Kinsey, et al, 1948, p. 197)*

The effects of the conventional sex code have been diverse and clearly adverse. Dr. Abram Kardiner, professor of psychiatry at Columbia University, has said that "there is no one living in our culture whose personality does not bear the imprint of sexual difficulties or character distortions from our form of sexual morality." (Kardiner, 1954, p. 150) Dr. Kardiner has said elsewhere that "neurosis and perversion are direct functions of the methods of sexual control, when they are induced and by what means this control is effected." (Kardiner, in Hoch & Zubin, 1949, p. 87)

George P. Murdock, an anthropologist who completed a cross-cultural study of some 250 societies, has said that "A comparative survey thus strongly suggests that our Puritanical sexual ethics is a luxury for which we pay a rather heavy price in organized vice, homosexuality, bestiality, crimes of sexual violence, and neurosis." (Murdock, in Hock & Zubin, 1949, p. 263) So the evidence continues to mount against the conventional sex morality and its untoward effects.

One of the most momentous effects of conventional sex morality is the tremendous guilt engendered in the individual as a result of being reared under such an unhealthy orientation. Erich Fromm, a psychoanalyst and social psychologist, has explained how this occurs:

> *"The most effective method for weakening the child's*
> *will is to arouse his sense of guilt. This is done early by*

making the child feel that his sexual strivings and their early manifestations are 'bad.' Since the child cannot help having sexual strivings, this method of arousing guilt can hardly fail. Once parents (and society represented by them) have succeeded in making the association of sex and guilt permanent, guilt feelings are produced to the same degree, and with the same constancy as sexual impulses occur. In addition, other physical functions are blighted by 'moral' considerations." (Fromm, 1947, pp. 155-156)

A great deal of hostility so prevalent in our society results from conventional upbringing in sexual matters. Wendell Johnson, a psychologist, has said that

"Not infrequently this hostility appears as a reaction to fundamentally sexual frustration. The moral codes of our culture are, in some homes and in some communities, quite brutally strict, as enforced. Permitted no clearly approved outlet for powerful natural drives, children tend to react with hatred of their parents and of other persons who frustrate them." (Johnson, 1946, p. 250)

Some of the diverse effects of conventional sex morality have well put by Grace Stuart in her definitive book <u>Conscience and Reason</u>, where she said:

"Were life more sensual it would be more good! And yet we still so often start our babies off in a world where we are half ashamed of suckling, half disgusted by excretion, half afraid of nakedness, and more than half

ashamed of sex.

We can neither be sensual ourselves nor allow others their sensuality. Neither enter the heaven of our earth, nor let those others in. So, having despised the lower, we seek fretfully and vainly for what we call the 'higher' things. Having poisoned the soil in which they grow we rail against the bitterness of the fruit." (Stuart, 1951, p. 202)

D. Why Conventional Sex Morality Needs to Be Replaced by Rational Sex Ethics

The foregoing presentation of conventional sex morality, how it arose from ancient religious beliefs, along with some of the unrealistic expectations of the conventional code, as well as some of the adverse effect of the conventional code, force the conclusion upon us that conventional sex morality needs to be replaced by more rational sex ethics. This conclusion is buttressed by the fact that a variety of scientists, working independently, from different points of view, and different specialties, have come to this same general conclusion. The many quotations from a large variety of specialists have been purposely included to show that this conclusion is not merely the point of view of a few radical writers, as the apologists for the conventional view would have us believe.

Sigmund Freud, speaking for the psychoanalysts, has said,

"We have found it impossible to give our support to conventional morality or to approve highly of the means by which society attempts to arrange the practical problems of sexuality in life. We can demonstrate with

ease that what the world calls its code of morals demands
more sacrifices than it is worth, and that its behavior is
neither dictated by honesty nor instituted with wisdom. "
(Freud, 1920, pp. 376-377)

J. M. Robertson, in his book <u>A Short History of Morals</u>, has said that

"The net outcome of official Christian ethics,
Catholic and Protestant alike, was the conception of sin
as an offense against Omnipotence, requiring supernatural
pardon, which required a supernatural sacrifice, which
required faith, which required grace, given by
Omnipotence in answer to prayer. The logical circle of
negation of human judgment was thus complete; and
human judgment, accordingly, was nominally excluded from
the fundamental process of deciding what was sin, or what
were sins, to begin with." (Robertson, 1920, pp. 186-187)

One of the needed tasks for the future, then, is to return sex ethics to human judgment.

Perhaps some will feel that this chapter has been too strong a condemnation of conventional sex morality. Some may feel that the conventional code has "evolved" from the "wisdom of the race," or some such formulation. This is, ultimately, a feeble attempt to justify in some fashion the conventional code. The anthropologist Robert Briffault has pointed out the error in such thinking:

"It is customary to regard those standards as the
mature fruit of accumulated human experience, as the
temperate conclusions of human wisdom. But it is not so.

> *They are the survival of what, in their original form, few*
> *would hesitate to pronounce as being the fanatical ravings*
> *of delirious minds." (Briffault, in Calverton &*
> *Schmalhausen, 1929, p. 49)*

As another student of the subject, Kinsey, has put it:

> *"Whether sexual acts are evaluated in terms of what*
> *is right or wrong (as the upper social level puts it), or*
> *what is natural or unnatural (as the lower social level*
> *considers it), the Hebraic and Christian concept of the*
> *reproductive function of sex lies back of both*
> *interpretations." (Kinsey, et al, 1948, p. 487)*

One of the fundamental reasons why conventional sex morality had better
be replaced is because of the supernatural assumptions underlying the
conventional code. As Homer W. Smith has concluded in his book <u>Man and
His Gods,</u>

> *"All human history reveals that transcendental*
> *metaphysics is not only futile but dangerous. Those who*
> *have foisted, frequently by not too honest means, their*
> *unsupported speculations upon the naive and gullible as*
> *truth have served to retard man's self-realization more*
> *than any other misfortune that has ever befallen him."*
> *(Smith, 1952, p. 443)*

Even Simon Doniger, editor of the book <u>Sex and Religion Today</u> (which
essentially defends the conventional Christian view), has stated that "It is
unfortunately true that religion all too frequently, in its attempts to control

the fires of sex, has tried to extinguish them altogether." (Doniger, 1953, p. vi)

This brings us to our final conclusion for this chapter, as bluntly put by the sociologist Harry Elmer Barnes:

> *"Heretofore religion has been regarded as the supreme custodian of sexual knowledge and the sovereign guide to sexual behavior; in the new order religion would have no part whatever in determining socially desirable sex conduct." (Barnes, in Calverton & Schmalhausen, 1929, p. 331)*

What shall be the basis of a more rational sex ethics rest upon then? In the next chapter we shall consider just this.

CHAPTER 1 REFERENCES

Bainton, Roland H. What Christianity Says About Sex, Love and Marriage. New York: Association Press, 1957.

Rainton, Roland H. "Christianity and Sex: An Historical Survey," pp. 17096 in Doniger, Simon (Editor). Sex and Religion Today. New York: Association Press, 1953.

Barnes, Harry Elmer. The Twilight of Christianity. New York: Vanguard Press, 129.

Barnes, Harry Elmer. "Sex in Education," pp. 285-348, in Calverton, V. F. & Schmalhausen, S. D. (Editors). Sex in Civilization. New York: Garden City, 1929.

Barnes, Harry Elmer. Society in Transition. New York: Prentice-Hall, 1939.

Blanshard, Paul. American Freedom and Catholic Power. Boston: Beacon Press, 1949.

Briffault, Robert. "Sex in Religion," pp. 31-52, in Calverton, V. F. & Schmalhausen, S. D. (Editors). Sex in Civilization. Garden City, N. Y.: Garden City, 1929.

Cavan, Ruth S. The American Family. New york: Crowell, 1953.

Cole, William Graham. Sex in Christianity and Psychoanalysis. New York: Oxford University Press, 1955.

Comfort, Alex. Sexual Behavior in Society. New York: Viking Press, 1950.

Ditzion, Sidney. Marriage, Morals and Sex in America. New York: Bookman, 1953.

Doniger, Simon (Editor). Sex and Religion Today. New York: Association Press, 1953.

Ellis, Albert. The American Sexual Tragedy. New York: Twayne, 1954.

Fletcher, Joseph. "A Moral Philosophy of Sex," in Doniger, Simon (Editor). Sex and Religion Today. New York: Association Press, 1953.

Freud, Sigmund. A General Introduction to Psychoanalysis. Garden City, N. Y.: Garden City, 1920.

Fromm, Erich. Man For Himself. New York: Rinehard, 1947.

Guyon, Rene. The Ethics of Sexual Acts. New York: Knopf, 1948.

Hiltner, Seward. Sex Ethics and the Kinsey Reports. New York: Association Press, 1953.

Johnson, Wendell. People In Quandries. New York: Harper, 1946.

Kardiner, Abram. Sex and Morality. New York: Bobbs-Merrill, 1954.

Kinsey, A. C., et al. Sexual Behavior in the Human Female. Philadelphia: Saunders, 1953.

Langdon-Davies, John. Sex, Sin and Sanctity. London: Gollancz, 1954.

Lerner, Max. America as a Civilization. New York: Simon & Schuster, 1957.

Mangasarian, M. M. The Bible Unveiled. Chicago: Independent Religious Society, Rationalist, 1911.

May, Geoffrey. Social Control of Sex Expression. New York: Morrow, 1931.

Murdock, George Peter. "The Social Regulation of Sexual

Behavior," pp. 526-266, in Hoch, P. H. & Zubin, J. (Editors). Psycho-sexual Development in Health and Disease. New York: Grune & Stratton, 1949.

Pittinger, W. Norman. The Christian View of Sexual Behavior. Greenwich, Conn.: Seabury Press, 1954.

Robertson, J. M. A Short History of Morals. London: Watts, 1920.

Smith, Homer W. Man and His Gods. Boston: Little, Brown, 1952.

Stuart, Grace. Conscience and Reason. New York: Macmillian, 1951.

Thompson, Clara. Psychoanalysis: Evolution and Development. New York: Hermitage House, 1950.

TIME, Sep. 30, 1957.

Wylie, Philip. "Is Love Out of Season?" (A Review of Robert Elliot Fitch's book, The Decline and Fall of Sex) "Saturday Review", August 3, 1957.

"Every human being, just because he exists, should have the right to as much (or as little), as varied (or as monotonous), as intense (or as mild), as enduring (or as brief) sex enjoyments as he prefers as long as, in the process of acquiring these preferred satisfactions, he does not needlessly, forcefully, or unfairly interfere with the sexual (or non-sexual) rights and satisfactions of others."
Albert Ellis (Sex Without Guilt,
1958, pp. 189-190)

CHAPTER 2
THE BASIC PRINCIPLES OF RATIONAL SEX ETHICS

A. Assumptions and Value Judgments

Back of most ethical systems lies a value judgment, more often implicit than explicit, about the essential nature of human beings. As Erich Fromm has said, "The value judgments we make determine our actions, and upon their validity rests our mental health and happiness." (Fromm, 1947, p. viii) If humans are thought of as inherently evil or bad, or even thought to have large amounts of evil in them which must be strictly controlled or constantly eradicated, the repressive and prohibitive sort of <u>morality</u> readily follows. The traditional view held that human nature was essentially depraved; human nature was thought of as warped by some supposed "original sin." These are <u>supernatural</u> assumptions.

However, the basic value judgment underlying the more rational sex <u>ethics</u> expounded here, which can be backed up by considerable <u>scientific</u> evidence, is that humans are fundamentally or essentially good by nature, given the proper environment in which to develop all of their normal potentialities and, for the most part, only develop aspects which have been termed bad as a result of their experiences in life, some of which are the results of the conventional sex morality which this book is intended to counter-act.

Erich Fromm, in his book <u>Man For Himself</u> (1947, p. 7), has shown that the sources of norms for ethical conduct may be found in man's nature itself; that ethical norms should be based upon man's inherent qualities, and the sources of norms for ethical conduct may be found in man's nature itself; that ethical norms should be based upon man's inherent qualities, and that violation of these norms results in mental and emotional disintegration. The sources of rational sex ethics, then, are natural rather than supernatural.

The function of a rational system of sex ethics would be to help individuals so order their lives (that is, their sexual attitudes and acts) so that each and every individual may realize, in so far as possible, his or her optimum development, with as little harm and interference to (and from) others, commensurate with this development. This is the overall purpose of a rational system of sex ethics.

A basic judgment of the author is that the evaluating part of the person, what is sometimes called the conscience (or among some psychotherapists, the superego), had better be eliminated and that ethical judgments in the sexual area, as in all others, and such value judgments as are necessary be based upon rational standards arrived at by the individual on the basis of the scientific approach rather than the traditional moralistic judgments and institutional prohibitions forced upon the child which later operates in an unconscious, irrational manner. (Ard, Living Without Guilt and/or Blame: Conscience, Superego and Psychotherapy, 1983) The balance of evidence seems to suggest that traditional institutional patterns of sexual conduct seem to aggravate the problems involved in such decisions rather than reduce them, and that "personal conduct, being the concern of persons, is best regulated, even in its difficulties, by the judgments of persons, however fallible or injudicious they may be. The power of prohibition to make men good is something sociology consistently fails to detect." (Comfort, 1950, pp. 114-115)

B. Purpose

The purpose behind the basic principles presented in this chapter is to help develop sex ethics based upon the psycho-physical actualities of the sexual nature of normal, mature human beings. The view put forth here is based upon the form of rationalism and humanism which seems to the author closest to the general approach of science: "that no form of sexual behavior can be regarded as unacceptable, sinful, or deserving of censure unless it has demonstrable ill effects on the individual who practices it, or on others." (Comfort, 1950, p. 16)

If the reader believes that human relations in the sexual area are essentially all right as they are presently (or would be all right if people would just follow the conventional code), he or she probably will not agree with the principles and statements to follow. But if the reader has followed the arguments presented so far (without throwing the book down), he or she probably believes by now at least that something significant and fundamental in the way of change in our sex ethics is vitally needed.

C. Contrast Between Authoritarian Morality and Humanistic Ethics

The humanistic ethics advocated herein differ from traditional, authoritarian morality in certain significant ways. As Fromm has carefully pointed out, authoritarian morality denies man's capacity to know what is good or bad; the norm given is always an authority transcending the individual.

> *"Such a system is based not on reason and knowledge but on awe of the authority and on the*

> *subject's feeling of weakness and dependence; the*
> *surrender of decision making to the authority results from*
> *the latter's magic power; its decisions can not and must*
> *not be questioned... authoritarian ethics answers the*
> *questions of what is good or bad primarily in terms of*
> *the interest of the authority, not the interest of the*
> *subject." (Fromm, 1947, p. 10)*

Thus authoritarian morality is necessarily exploitative.

Humanistic ethics, on the other hand, are based on the principle that only humans themselves can determine the criterion for good and evil, not an authority transcending them. "Good" is thus what is good for humans and "evil" is what is detrimental to humans; the sole criterion of ethical value being humans' welfare. (Cf. Fromm, 1947, p. 13)

Thus, in this context, and throughout the present book, morality is the term used to denote values based on authoritarian ideas, religious assumptions, mystical premises, faith unfounded on fact, supernatural presumptions, and so forth. While ethics refers to value judgments that can be checked out, verified or falsified in an empirical, scientific manner and serve the values of human beings.

D. Some Fundamental Principles

The foregoing paragraphs have covered what might be termed the basic assumptions, presuppositions, or value judgments underlying the rational sex ethics advocated in this book (along with a brief discussion of the contrast between authoritarian morality and humanistic or rational sex ethics). Any discussion such as offered in this book must start somewhere and therefore must start with some assumptions. It would take several books to justify these assumptions, here we can only say that the assumptions can be justified by turning to the scientific evidence offered by the various scientific specialists referred to throughout the book. The reader is urged to check the assumptions out by reading further in the books cited.

As one of the best justifications of rationality in general, one may turn with profit to the philosopher John Kekes and his book A Justification of Rationality (1976), where he says:

> "The conception implicit in the theory of rationality
> is that rationality is a method for achieving what is
> supposed to be in one's best interest. There are other
> methods, but rationality is by far the best. The claim is
> not that only a rational policy is possible, but only that
> such a policy will be in what a person regards as his best
> interest. So the justification will recommend itself only to
> those who do wish to act in what they think of as their
> best interest, whatever that interest is conceived to be.
> Of course, there are people who due to ignorance,
> ineptitude, psychological problems, or conscious decision
> fail to do what they regard as being in their best
> interest. Such people are paradigmatically irrational."
> (John Kekes, 1976, p. 165)

Now we turn to judgments on another level, the basic principles upon which rational sex ethics may be said to rest. By "principles" we mean fundamental generalized statements upon which later, more specific ethical judgments are based or derived from, as it were. These basic principles are again based upon scientific evidence from the various pertinent disciplines.

They are not "revelations," nor intuitive hunches or "insights" but simply the more fundamental ideas upon which rational sex ethics are based. They are naturalistic rather than supernatural statements. They are not "proven" in the sense of "absolute" certainty; no empirical judgments of any science ever are. They are based upon scientific thinking and research and several scientific authorities are cited for them. Naturally, however, no matter how many authorities were cited, a reader might disagree with any particular principle or statement. The authorities quoted are not cited as "proof" of any principle but merely to lead the reader to other sources where he or she might verify these statements and see the evidence for them.

These principles or statements are not intended as "final" in any sense either. They are merely the best ideas we have from science today. As newer evidence is forthcoming, rational sex ethics will always be willing to incorporate such new knowledge into its considerations.

Although rational sex ethics are attempts to make objectively valid judgments, "objectively valid" is not identical with "absolute." For instance a judgment may be a statement of probability, an approximation, an hypothesis which can be valid and at the same time not "absolute" since it is established on perhaps limited evidence and is always subject to future refinement if and when newly discovered facts warrant it. (Fromm, 1947, p. 16)

A rational sex code thus will, in so far as it is rational, be based upon an understanding of sexual matters that is directly rooted in factual observation. As Albert Ellis has stated, it will therefore be "a flexible code that has possibilities of changing as new findings about sex, love and marriage are discovered by clinicians and scientists." (Ellis, 1954, p. 252)

In an abbreviated form the following six principles will be discussed: (1) the legitimacy of sex, (2) the right of sexual freedom (3) the equality of all in sexual matters, (4) the necessary absence of force or coercion into one pattern, (5) the frequency and character of sexual acts considered as private matters of personal hygiene, and (6) no sexual act being banned unless its consequences are harmful.

With these basic principles in mind we will turn to more detailed ethical discussions on specific sexual problems in later chapters. Now let us spell out as explicitly as possible the basic principles of rational sex ethics.

(1) Legitimacy of Sex

One of the attributes of every normal human being is his or her sexual nature. In other words, sex is a natural, essential, legitimate part of every normal human being. This is the first basic principle of rational sex ethics. This may seem to some readers to be such an obvious thing to say that they may wonder why it is even necessary to say it at all. But of all the different aspects of human nature, the one part that has been most consistently denied normal expression in our culture has been the sexual nature of human beings.

As has been pointed out in the preceding chapter, sexual pleasure has been denied legitimate expression by conventional sex morality. Rational sex ethics, however, will consider sexual satisfaction as legitimate and desirable. As Guyon has put it, sexual pleasure "is no less necessary than is sufficient and agreeable food to a full, healthy, balanced, and happy life." (Guyon, 1950, p. 149)

A rational sex code will be based on the premise that men and women have biological sex needs. It will try to see that these are satisfied as fully and as easily as possible, providing that they do not bring harm to other individuals. (Albert Ellis, 1954, pp. 251-252)

If the gratification of sexual desire is considered legitimate (as legitimate as other psychological and bodily needs), then it would seem to follow that any method for achieving such gratification would also be legitimate, barring only those methods that may harm the partner or be inflicted without his or her consent. (Guyon, 1950, p.35)

It is the contention of the humanistic point of view expounded in this book that society, through the influence of supernatural religious beliefs, has gone too far in forcing the repression of sex. Consideration of the full consequences of this repression of sex forces the conclusion that there are psychological limits beyond which it would be better if society did not press the individual. The repression of the sexual impulse leads to personal unhappiness and disease. (Ard, Treating Psychosexual Dysfunction, 1974)

Once it is granted that any reasonable system of sex ethics had better be in accord with human nature, and then it is admitted that sex is an essential part of that human nature, it follows that satisfactory arrangements had better be allowed for in any rational sex ethics, i.e., to provide for the adequate expression of this natural, normal part of all human beings. Rather than assuming that sex is a sinful, evil, dangerous part of the human personality, rational sex ethics would more reasonably assume that all human beings are entitled to the natural expression of their sexual nature, provided only that they do not force their attentions on others, or cause any harm by their sexual endeavors. In the naturalistic context which rational sex ethics assumes, no supernatural assumptions about God's plans need be made. We do not have to speculate about who does or does not have a pipeline direct to

Heaven and thus has access to God's plans and any "commandments" that go along with His plans.

(2) The Right of Sexual Freedom

The most succinct statement of the second basic principle underlying the system of sex ethics presented herein may be stated in the form of a right which each individual is entitled to, granting the above premises: Each man, woman and child has the right to the freedom necessary for the natural unfolding of every one of his or her normal faculties of mind and body that can contribute to his or her happiness. This entails the right to the free and equal development, and exercise thereof, of his or her sexual capacities by each individual.

"Free and equal development" does not imply that each individual must have exactly the same sexual life as every other individual. Freedom and equality are basic concepts in the democratic philosophy. But the concept of equality does not imply that all people are equal in every respect, or that they must or should be. The concept of equality, rightly conceived, means that all people have equal rights to the things that bring their own self-realization or optimum development. Humans are only equal in the sense that they all have the same rights.

(3) Equality of All in Sexual Matters

This discussion of freedom and equality leads us right into the third basic principle of rational sex ethics. It should hardly be necessary to spell out a third principle in this respect but since traditional views have ruled against miscegenation and inter-marriages between people of differing religion, a rational sex code would be a code that does not discriminate on any basis of race, creed, religion, color, or other such attribute but is generally the same for all members of the community in this regard. (Albert Ellis, 1954, p. 252)

The basic inalienable right of every individual to a free, responsible exercise of his or her normal sexual nature has been ably expressed by Guyon in the following fashion:

> "Everybody has the right to exercise quite freely his own preferences in matters of sex, so long as he is guilty of no violence of deceit to others; the right to sexual satisfaction is just an inalienable as the right to eat." (Guyon, 1948, p. 139)

(4) The Absence of Force or Coercion into One Pattern

The fourth basic principle of rational sex ethics is that no individual should be forced or coerced into a pattern of sexual living which goes against his normal sexual nature. There is no one pattern of sexual living which is identical for all human beings, although there is a general or over-all similarity to the sexual lives of psychologically mature individuals which may be taken as tentative guides but not rigidly and minutely followed as patterns. (Maslow, 1953)

The rational sex ethics of a truly civilized people had better be, above all,

> "a non-rigid, non-traditionalized, objective code which makes no assumption that only one particular method of sex-marriage living is right, good, and proper, nor that all individuals in a given society must live rigorously in conformity with this one all-inclusive mode of living." (Albert Ellis, 1954, p. 254)

The concept of the freedom of each individual to choose the kind of sexual life which is most satisfying to that person (i.e., which leads to the person's own optimum development), within the limits set by rational sex ethics, is one of the most fundamental of all the basic principles of rational sex ethics. Guyon, who first formulated the most extensive statement of the legitimacy of sexual acts, has stated that "we must not forget that our conception of the legitimacy of sexual acts demands throughout the fullest respect for the liberty of others and the free consent (uncomplicated by any element of violence or deceit) of the sexual partner." (Guyon, 1948, p. 341)

Anyone who has grasped the importance of sex throughout life, and has realized the risks which arise from the faulty handling of sex will have to agree with Guyon that it is of the first importance for person who wish to guide their lives intelligently to take a definite line upon this question of sexual freedom.

> *"Instead of obeying blindly and without independent thought traditional guides who are apt to contradict one another, he should, deliberately and with full awareness, adopt a sexual policy of his own which will enable him to regulate his life in accordance with principles he considers sound." (Guyon, 1950, p. 52)*

Taking the principles enumerated so far, we may say that rational sex ethics affirm the right of the individual to the greatest possible freedom of development and action compatible with the equal rights of others to similar development and action.

(5) The Frequency and Character of Sexual Acts
Considered as Private Matters of Personal Hygiene

The fifth basic principle of rational sex ethics states that the frequency and character of sexual acts are better considered as matters for individual regulation and as problems of personal hygiene, in the same way as are the activities of all the other bodily functions. This principle has been previously stated by Guyon (1950, p. 137) It should be clear that this principle is obviously in great contrast to the traditional way of evaluating sexual activities in terms of sin or some other theological concept.

When concepts like sin (or one's soul being in danger) are to be weighed in peoples' ethical dilemmas about sexual matters, then these supernatural concepts are arbitrarily decided by someone who maintains that he has a direct line to God's commandments. But when it is a question of personal hygiene, then it can be resolved in a naturalistic, scientific fashion (by consulting a physician, psychiatrist, psychologist or counselor).

(6) No Sexual Act Is Banned Unless Its Consequences Are Harmful

The sixth basic principle is that no sexual act is to be banned or discouraged unless it specifically, needlessly, gratuitously, and forcibly results in one individual's harming another individual or individuals (or oneself). (Albert Ellis, The American Sexual Tragedy, 1954, p. 251)

This principle states the limits under which rational sex ethics would operate. As should be obvious, just because one is for sexual freedom, it does not follow (as some would have us believe) that one is for sexual license.

E. Some Implications of Rational Sex Ethics

The value of rational sex ethics rests to a great extent upon these fundamental principles which, in their aggregate, allow each individual the freedom which is essential to the optimum development of his or her potentialities. These principles assure everyone that, within the limits of as little harm and interference to others commensurate with the optimum development of all, each person is free to pursue his or her own optimum development, his or her own sexual life, free from the interference of others. This freedom is basic to rational sex ethics because it is only through such freedom that humans can develop all of their human potentialities.

Albert Ellis has noted an important point when he has said that a rational sex code

> "should not be based on any arbitrary assumptions concerning the intrinsic and necessary linking of sex, love, marriage, and child-raising desires, needs and functions. While recognizing the desirability, perhaps, of intertwining such functions in certain (and perhaps most) instances, it should not insist on the necessity of their connection for all persons at all places at all times."
> (Albert Ellis, 1954, p. 251)

The above principles mean, among other things, that the person with low sex drive is not expected to have the same pattern of sexual living as the person with stronger drives, nor vice versa. Every person cannot be expected to marry by a certain age, have a given number of children, and so to pattern his or her life in any prescribed fashion. This means, as Margaret Mead has said, that

> "we can have no clear vision of a final form which

> *we want society to take; for the minute that we have*
> *such a vision we begin to educate, cajole, force people,*
> *identified living human beings, to fit into the pattern*
> *which we have conceived as good for them." (Mead,*
> *1942,. p. 189)*

Our job is rather "towards creating instead conditions within which unidentified individuals may act of their own free will." (Mead, 1942, p. 187)

> *"If we turn our attention towards processes, towards*
> *directions, and away from fixed plans into which we*
> *attempt to fit living human beings, we deal immediately*
> *with an open-ended system, a system in which we cannot*
> *know what the outcome will be. We have inevitably*
> *accorded to human beings, the human beings of the*
> *future, the right to a destiny which lies in their hands,*
> *not in ours." (Mead, 1942, p. 190)*

Also, we have not laid down their future for them: we have only said

> *"We think that in this direction lies a freer life, a*
> *life in which more of the energies of human beings can*
> *be used than have ever been used before. We have set*
> *your footsteps on this path, we have equipped you to*
> *think well and to feel sensitively - what you make of*
> *your future lies in your hands." (Mead, 1942, pp. 190-191)*

No one will be forced to avail himself or herself of the sexual opportunities which may seem to some to be granted too readily in the atmosphere of sexual freedom which would prevail under a more rational system of sex ethics. If an individual wishes to go through life without any use whatsoever of his or her sexual capacities, he or she is free to do so under this system, although one would suspect that there was something the matter with such an individual. If the knowledge that sexual functioning is normal (and thus expected in some sense) failed to free the individual sufficiently to function, perhaps such knowledge would help such a person to seek psychological counsel. But even this last step is up to him or her, under the freedom of rational sex ethics. As long as one does not harm or interfere with the freedom of others to develop their own optimum, each individual is free to lead the sexual life he or she prefers.

It will be readily seen that rational sex ethics are based upon the study of man (i.e., the sciences of psychology, anthropology, psychiatry, sociology, sexology, etc.), rather than upon any supposedly "holy" book or supposed revelation. Rational sex ethics are concerned about the happiness and self-fulfillment of human beings in this life and are not concerned with any supposed future life. Sexual actions are evaluated in terms of their consequences and not in relation to any supposedly "divine" commandments. It is a naturalistic, rather than a supernatural orientation. A rational sex code would be based on intelligent and rational thinking about sex matters,

> "and should not be beholden to irrational, superstitious, highly emotionalized, religious, or other non-logical attitudes. If sectarian groups wish to force on their members traditional, conventional, non-logical sex-marriage ethics, they should be permitted to do so; but they should not be allowed to foist on all members of society any of their own sectarian viewpoints and practices as, for example, the Catholic Church tries to do

today in opposing laws for legalized birth controls and education." (Albert Ellis, 1954, pp. 252-253)

Through a study of human nature as it naturally unfolds in the psychologically mature, we can best determine what ought to be. (Maslow, 1950) In other words, by living in accordance with humans' true nature, humans can achieve goodness.

Essentially, the fundamental thesis underlying this book is the same as that stated by Wendell Johnson in his book, People in Quandries (1946, p. 45), and that is simply that science, clearly understood, can be used from moment to moment in everyday life, and that it provides a sound basis for warmly human and efficient living. It may seem to some readers that there is something almost bold in Wendell Johnson's proposition that the method of science not only provides a means of investigating personality, but also represents in itself the pattern of behavior that constitutes normal personality. (Johnson, 1946, pp. 382-383) But this is the fundamental proposition of Wendell Johnson's book and also of general semantics. (Rapoport, 1953) "The method of science is the method of sanity." (Johnson, 1946, pp. 382-382)

Now let us turn to more specific areas in human life where sex has been a problem and the source of much anxiety and guilt. First, let us consider sex in childhood.

CHAPTER 2 REFERENCES

Ard, Ben N., Jr. Treating Psychosexual Dysfunction. New York: Jason Aronson, 1974.

Ard, Ben N., Jr. "The Conscience or Superego in Marriage Counseling." pp. 61-67 in Ard, Ben N., Jr. & Ard, C. C. (Editors) Handbook of Marriage counseling. Palo Alto: Science & Behavior Books, 2nd edition, 1976.

Ard, Ben N., Jr. Living Without Guilt and/or Blame: Conscience, Superego and Psychotherapy. New York: American Liberty Publishing, Inc., 2nd edition, 1988.

Comfort, Alex. Sexual Behavior in Society. New York: Viking Press, 1950.

Ellis, Albert. The American Sexual Tragedy. New York: Twayne, 1954.

Ellis, Albert. Sex Without Guilt. New York: Lyle Stuart, 1958.

Fromm, Erich. Man For Himself. New York: Rinehart, 1947.

Guyon, Rene. The Ethics of Sexual Acts. New York: Knopf, 1948.

Guyon, Rene. Sexual Freedom. New York: Knopf, 1950.

Johnson, Wendell. People in Quandries. New York: Harper, 1946.

Kekes, John. A Justification of Rationality. Albany: State University of New York, 1976.

Maslow, A. H. "Self-actualizing People: A Study in Psychological Health," pp. 11-34 in Wolff, Werner (Editor) Personality: Symposium No. 1: Values in Personality Research. New York: Grune & Stratton, 1950.

Maslow, A. H. "Love in Healthy People," pp. 57-93 in Montague,

58

Ashley (Editor) <u>The Meaning of Love</u>. New York: Julian, 1953.

Mead, Margaret. <u>And Keep Your Powder Dry</u>. New York: Morrow, 1942.

Rapoport, Anatol. <u>Operational Philosophy</u>. New York: Harper, 1953.

"As a child rearing measure, guilt-conditioning is an expedient, over-generalized substitute for more rational teaching by demonstration, precept, and explanation. In time we may even be able to discard the superego idea."
Donald J. Holmes (<u>Psychotherapy</u>, 1972, p. 220)

CHAPTER 3
CHILDREN AND SEX

Before taking up the matter of sex and children, one matter needs to be cleared up somewhat as a prefatory note. This matter is the acceptance of every child as a human being with rights equal to those of other children. According to one authority (McCary, 1973, p. 452), 33% of all firstborn children in the United States are conceived out of wedlock.

Under the conventional sex code many children are condemned, before they are even born, to social ostracism and a life devoid of their natural and normal rights by being classified as "illegitimate." Blameless children are thus unjustifiably saddled with the blame which society also put upon their parents. It is now recognized by serious thinkers that no useful purpose is served by stigmatizing children born out of wedlock as "illegitimate." (Bayles, in Baker & Ellistron, 1975, p. 200) The harm to children alone, to say nothing of the parents, which results from society's attitude toward those children born out of wedlock is incalculable.

One of the most serious results of this conventional attitude is the mental suffering felt by so-called "illegitimate" children over their status. The attitude of society is not merely that of "moral" condemnation but also includes legal penalties. The history of common law on this subject is a sorry thing to behold. As the jurist Morris Ploscowe has put in his book <u>Sex and the Law</u>,

> "*The bastard was kin to no one and could inherit from nobody, not even from his own mother, for he was not deemed to be the lawful child of his own mother. He was entitled to support from neither the mother nor the father. He was legally adrift at birth. ....At common law, it was indeed 'tough to be a bastard'.*" *(Ploscowe, 1951, pp. 102-103)*

Such language may appear too strong to some but as a simple matter of fact the common law of illegitimacy was obviously brutal. For those who think that such attitudes no longer prevail in our courts, Morris Ploscowe says,

> "*Our modern lawyers, however, seek to cloak unpleasant social facts with fancy names. Bastards are now called illegitimate, out-of-wedlock or natural children. Proceedings to establish paternity are called affiliation or paternity proceedings. But so little concerned is the modern law with substance that it has frequently neglected to provide that the fact of illegitimacy should not be put upon birth certificates.*" *(Ploscowe, 1951, p. 133)*

Under a more rational sex code, all children would be considered legitimate and thus another teaching of the conventional code eliminated as unjust and untenable. As McCary has put it,

> "*It seems only fair, and it is certainly sound reasoning insofar as contributing to the mental health of*

the population is concerned, that the states should establish more adequate laws to protect the illegitimate child." (McCary, 1973, p. 456)

If, as Ploscowe says, the law is

"to get away from the timid, half-hearted approach to problems of illegitimacy, if it is to provide a set of rules that meet modern needs, then it must make a sharp break with common-law conceptions." (Ploscowe, 1951, p. 133)

Fortunately, some states have made steps in this direction. But in only two states -- Arizona and North Dakota -- are all children considered legitimate and accorded equal rights. (McCary, 1973, p. 455) Obviously what is needed is an acceptance by all of the inadequacy of our conventional attitudes on this matter and a clear stand on the principle that all children are legitimate.

Sexual Manifestations Among Children

The next step, from the point of view of rational sex ethics, is to accept the natural sexual manifestations which occur in normal children as they are growing up. It is to the great merit of Sigmund Freud, the founder of psychoanalysis, that he revealed the error in the early conventional views about sex in childhood. One can accept the great contributions of Freud in showing the extent of sexual manifestations in childhood without necessarily having to subscribe to certain of his theoretical views, such as the perversity of childhood sexuality, or the sol-called universality of the Oedipus complex, for example. Freud said

"It is commonly believed that the sexual instinct is

lacking in children, and only begins to arise in them when the sexual organs mature. This is a grave error...It is so easy to correct it by observation that one can only wonder how it can ever have arisen. As a matter of fact, the new-born infant brings sexuality with it into the world...and only very few children would seem to escape some kind of sexual activity and sexual experience before puberty." (Freud, 1924, II, p. 38)

The facts are, then, that sex manifests itself in many forms from birth onward. (Sears, 1947, pp. 23-37, 135-136; Frank, 1949, pp. 143-158; Henry, 1949, pp. 91-101) The complete sexual act with resulting progeny is, of course, not usually possible until puberty or adolescence but that is about all that can be said for the traditional viewpoint. The traditional point of view simply refused to see any sexual manifestations in children except as abnormal perversities. The traditional view was to some degree oblivious to "sex" in children because it practically equated sex with reproduction.

This confusion of procreation with sex may account for a lot of the oversights of the traditional view. Sex was thought of as practically synonymous with reproduction while in actuality reproduction is a secondary or derivative result of some sex, and only then at certain times and under specific conditions. The primary function of sex is thus the pleasure or play function rather than mere reproduction.

This primary function of sex was either overlooked entirely by the traditional view or, if it was admitted that sex served a pleasure function, it was imply denied that this was a valuable function. The pleasure function was specifically what the traditional viewpoint railed against as "sinful." In fact, sex as distinguished from reproduction was sinful in just about any of its manifestations, that is to say, from the traditional point of view. This is perhaps why practically any sexual manifestations in children were either not recognized as sexual or, at the least, first frowned upon, then severely suppressed by most parents and teachers who subscribed to the traditional point of view. Sexual manifestations in childhood, according to the traditional view, were not considered "normal."

As a matter of actual fact, however, normal boys and girls show sexual manifestations from their earliest days, as is apparent to any objective observer. The psychologist Robert Sears, after his survey of objective studies of psychoanalytic concepts, stated that "sexual behavior in children has been shown to be exceedingly common." (Sears, 1947, p. 136) Kinsey and his associates have brought forth much objective evidence of the extent of sexual behavior in childhood. (Kinsey, et al, 1948, pp. 157-192; 1943, pp. 101-131) This interdisciplinary team of research workers came to this conclusion:

> "These data on the sexual activities of younger males provides an important substantiation of the Freudian view of sexuality as a component that is present in the human animal from the earliest infancy, although it gives no support to the Freudian concept of a pre-genital stage of generalized erotic response that precedes more specific genital activity; nor does it show any necessity for a sexually latent or dormant period in the later adolescent years, except as such inactivity results from parental and social repressions of the growing child." (Kinsey, et al, 1948, p. 180; Cf., also, brief review in Kinsey, 1953, p. 103)

Among the many manifestations of sex among children are such activities as playing with their genitals in infancy, which later develops into masturbation, sexual play and exhibition of their genitals. These manifestations are very common among children.

While every act of playing with their genitals might not be termed masturbation (certainly much of this handling of genitals by infants is somewhat accidental and exploratory at first), nevertheless this behavior soon develops into what must be called masturbation. Masturbation is thus to be expected in most children in our culture as a normal manifestation of the average child's combination of curiosity and experimentation, coupled with a normal sexual nature. Masturbation in very young children seems to be largely of an exploratory nature, a getting acquainted with their body and its functions. Later on in childhood masturbation may serve other psychological functions, for example when children are under stress they may masturbate as a sort of substitute gratification or release of tension. Seen in this light it follows that masturbation is not harmful but rather a normal, expected manifestation in our children.

The late Dr. Norman Haire, formerly editor of the English periodical The Journal of Sex Education, has stated that

"Children should not be alarmed by false teaching about masturbation. Masturbation is a normal physiological phenomenon. It is a form of sex-play which may be expected in most normal children..." (Haire, 1927, p. xiii)

In one of the most comprehensive articles published on masturbation, Lester Dearborn states unequivocally that "Masturbation, according to the best medical authorities, causes no harm physically or mentally. Any harm resulting from masturbation is caused entirely by worry or by a sense of guilt due to misinformation." (Dearborn, in Fishbein & Burgess, 1948, p. 366)

Sexual Play

Our culture is one of a minority of cultures wherein adults attempt to deny young children any form of sexual expression. (Ford & Beach, 1951, p. 180) As Ford and Beach have pointed out,

> *"Although the strictness with which the moral code is enforced varies considerably from one social class to another, a more or less concerted attempt to prevent children from any form of sex play continues well into adolescence and up to the time of marriage." (Ford & Beach, 1951, p. 185)*

Although this is the prevailing attitude in our culture there is still considerable sexual play among children, although many adults may not realize this fact. (Kinsey, et al, 1948, p. 169 and Figure 25; 1943, p. 111 and Figure 6)

Many adults do not recognize that children's games commonly referred to as "playing house" or "mamma and Papa" or "doctor" may have more of a sexual connotation than many adults would like to admit. Kinsey, et al, point out that a considerable portion of children's sex play is a product of curiosity concerning the playmate's anatomy. (Kinsey, et al, 1953, p. 108) Thus, for example, genital exhibition has occurred in 99 per cent of the pre-adolescent sex play among the females interviewed in Kinsey's study. (Kinsey, et al, 1953, p. 111)

Under a society based on a more rational sex ethics, the tendency of children to exhibit the naked body would be considered natural. Sexual play which involves exhibiting themselves or observing others is based, in our culture, upon sexual curiosity, which is a legitimate interest, if we accept the principles of rational sex ethics. In fact, this sort of curiosity and the exhibition of their nudity among small children, if coupled with sound sex education, may positively prevent later misunderstandings or disturbances when nudity is encountered.

As the psychologist Hugo Beigel has pointed out, children frequently satisfy their sexual curiosity by looking at nudes in pictures. (Beigel, 1952, p. 2569) And, as he says, "There is no good reason to object to this." For "nudity in art is not immoral." (Beigel, 1952, p. 259); nor is nudity per se immoral elsewhere, we might add. Parents can prevent children turning to what the parents may consider pornographic or "obscene" literature or pictures by having copies of famous works of art on the walls or in books available to the children.

Despite the overwhelming evidence (Kinsey, et al, 1948, 1953; Ford & Beach, 1951) that sex play in children is perfectly normal and natural, this is one of the hardest points for many adults in our culture to accept, particularly parents. Samuel Schmalhausen has commented on this point:

"*A wise parent or teacher looks upon the child as possessing erotic personality, and therefore as capable of many little experimental moods and tentatives toward experience that can do no harm if they are construed as playful and natural. I suppose the most difficult and the most necessary lesson for civilized persons to learn is a certain good-humored and scientifically innocent*

acceptance of nature as natural." (Schmalhausen, in
Calverton & Schmalhausem, 1930, p. 284)

He states further that "If we are sufficiently mature to realize that sex must be utterly reconceived in a complete dissociation from sin or ugliness or vulgarity or shame, we shall be well prepared to be wise friends of children." (Schmalhausen, in Calverton & Schmalhausen, 1930, p. 284) And, in conclusion, "One of the profoundest indictments against the home, as we know it, is its astonishing inability to surround sex with an atmosphere of sweetness and dignity and gladness." (Schmalhausen, in Calverton & Schmalhausen, 1930, p. 284)

The opposite philosophy may be seen in certain other cultures, for example, among the Trobrianders, Samoans, and Marquesans. The difference in attitude toward sex, and childhood sexuality in particular, is significant. "In these sexually free cultures,children are permitted to engage in sexplay and to develop their sexual function as early and as rapidly as their natural development permits..." (Folsom, 1943, p.79) In our sex-repressive society the custom is to restrain and postpone the development of this sexual behavior. Of course, this is commonly "justified" by the idea that the general development of the child is thereby safeguarded and thus prepared for a better sex life after maturity. However, as the sociologist Joseph Kirk Folsom has stated,

"recent studies upon sexually free cultures have cast
a heavy doubt upon this assumption. In those societies
sexual behavior pervades life from childhood on, and it is
difficult to see what is thereby lost. The repressive
character of our sexual philosophy goes much deeper than

a condemnation of sex outside marriage. It is essentially a declaration of the unworthiness of sex." (Folsom, 1943, p. 79)

Lest the reader feel that sex play is relatively unimportant in considerations regarding rational sex ethics, let us turn to some of the conclusions of Ford and Beach, an anthropologist and psychologist, respectively, who studied 190 different societies:

"The evolutionary data strongly suggest that human sexual patterns are not completely organized on a strictly inherited level. Instead, it is highly probable that practice is essential to complete arousal and particularly to satisfactory expression of sexual excitement. It follows, therefore, that if they are ever to derive maximal satisfaction from sexual relations, individuals who are reared under conditions that prevent or seriously reduce experimentation and practice during childhood and adolescence will be forced to go through the essential learning processes after adulthood.

This type of adjustment may be exceedingly difficult for young adults of either sex, particularly if they belong to a society that includes manifold sexual inhibitions in the developing individual. The man or woman who learned during childhood and adolescence that it was 'wrong' to examine or stimulate his or her own genitals, that it was even 'worse' to have any contact with those of another

person, and, particularly, that attempts at heterosexual
relations were immoral, is expected to reverse completely
at least some of these attitudes on the wedding night or
shortly thereafter. This expectation is difficult to fulfill.
If the initial lessons have been well learned, the
unlearning is bound to take a long time and may never be
completed." (Ford & Beach, 1951, pp. 195-196)

The important lesson we can learn from studying other cultures is that "a society which permits extensive sex play in childhood and adolescence may thereby increase the chances that sexual relations in marriage will be pleasant and mutually satisfying." (Ford & Beach, 1951, p. 197)

Sex Education

If children are to be prepared to function adequately in the sexual sphere, sex education must start at a much earlier age than has been customary in the conventional approach to this matter. Sex education, in so far as anything approximating it may be said to have been offered, traditionally was not even thought of usually until children had reached adolescence. In many cases girls were not prepared for this important aspect of their lives until they were about to be married. This approach to sex education was based, among other things, the erroneous notion that sex as such did not enter into the "normal" person's life until adulthood, when it supposedly burst forth in full bloom. In the female of the species it was expected that even then sexual thoughts would not enter her head, if she were "properly brought up," until marriage was at hand.

Rational sex ethics, along with the necessary facts of sexual psychology, anatomy and physiology, had better be presented to young people in order to enable them to deal rightly with all sexual events to which everyone is naturally liable (and so far as possible without injury either to themselves or to others). Young people can also learn about sex more easily if they start the process before they have already invested a lot of emotions in the sexual arena.

While sex educators have usually acknowledged that sex education should start in the home, when they have conducted sex education in the schools, they have all too often treated students as the more conservative parents would, to be on the "safe" side. (Ard, in Farber & Wilson, 1967, p. 81) This has resulted in sex educators unfortunately feeling it is their responsibility to teach, counsel, advise and exemplify "the accepted standards of morality," (i.e., conventional morality).

We had better avoid the sanctimonious, sacred, saccharine, sentimental approach to sex education which has been with us in this culture for so long. Instead of the single minded prohibitions and scare techniques so common, a more rational, opening-up approach which allows for different conclusions and solutions would seem a more enlightened approach. (Kirkendall, 1950) In other words, it would be better to get away from sex education which emphasizes the reproductive, repressive, religious approach. Essentially this is a suggestion that if we want our sex education to be better and more effective in the future than it has been in the past, then we had better change the underlying value assumptions from those of our traditional, moralistic sex code to a more rational, pluralistic and humanistic sex ethics.

Today tolerance for heterodoxy has declined to an unprecedented low level, what with attacks from the radical right on mental health, the schools in general, and particularly on anything having to do with sex. Family life education is usually considered a "frill" in these attacks and thus the first thing to be eliminated. When sex education is advocated by professional people, the frequent response is: the community, administrators and parents, or the churches, will oppose it. Letting this excuse buffalo us, we continue to let our young people down, year after year, by failing to provide an adequate sex education for them. Certainly many of the problems with regard to sex education would be potentially resolvable if people could only become free of their moralistic judgments regarding sex.

Does this mean that we should, therefore, not make any value judgments at all, as some cultural and ethical relativists maintain? Not at all. (Ard, in Ard, 1975, pp. 351-356) We shall continue to make ethical or value judgments, but our newer knowledge of human values shows that these value judgments have better be based on scientific evidence, reality, clear logical thinking, and the nature of human nature, not supernatural, moralistic considerations. (Maslow, 1959)

We do not have to abandon sex education to peer groups (that is academic jargon for the locker room), nor to the mass media (with its TV attitudes, Ann Landers, et al, in the newspapers, and the "Reader's Digest" approaches to sex). The cost of naivete of mis-education is as bad as that arising from no education. (Vincent, in Farber & Wilson, 1967)

CHAPTER 3 REFERENCES

Ard, Ben. "Do As I Do, Be As I Am: The Bruising Conflict," pp.
78-88, in Farber, Seymour M. & Wilson,Roger H. L. (Editors) <u>Sex</u>
<u>Education & the Teenager</u>. Berkeley: Diablo Press, 1967.

Ard, Ben N., Jr. "Are All Middle-class Values Bad?", pp. 351-356, in Ard, Ben
N., Jr. (Editor) <u>Counseling and Psychotherapy: Classics on Theories and</u>
<u>Issues</u>. Palo Alto: Science & Behavior Books, revised edition, 1975.

Bayles, Michael D. "Marriage, Love, and Procreation," pp. 190-266, in Baker,
Robert & Elliston, Frederick (Editors) <u>Philosophy & Sex</u>. Buffalo:
Prometheus Books, 1975.

Beigel, Hugo G. <u>Encyclopedia of Sex Education</u>. New York:
William Penn, 1952.

Dearborn, Lester. "Masturbation," pp. 356-367, in Fishbein,
Morris & Burgess, E. W. (Editors) <u>Successful Marriage</u>. Garden City, N.
Y.: Doubleday, 1948.

Folsom, Joseph Kirk. <u>The Family and Democratic Society</u>. New
York: Wiley, 1943.

Ford, C. S. & Beach, F. A. <u>Patterns of Sexual Behavior</u>. New
York: Harper, 1951.

Frank, Richard L. "Childhood Sexuality", pp. 143-158, in Hock,
Ph. H. & Zubin, J. (Editors) Psychosexual Development in Health and
Disease. New York: Grune & Stratton, 1949.

Freud, Sigmund. "The Sexual Enlightenment of Children," pp. 36-44, Volume
II, <u>Collected Papers</u>. London: Hogarth, 1924.

Haire, Norman. "Introduction," in Bauer, Bernhard. <u>Woman and</u>
<u>Love</u>. New York: Liveright, 1927.

Henry, Jules. "The Social Function of Child Sexuality in Pilaga
Indian Culture," pp. 91-101, in Hoch, P. H. & Zubin, J. (Editors)
Psychosexual Development in Health and Disease. New York: Grune &
Stratton, 1949.

Holmes, Donald J. Psychotherapy. Boston: Little, Brown, 1972.

Kinsey, A. C., et al. Sexual Behavior in the Human Male.
Philadelphia: Saunders, 1948.

Kinsey, A. C., et al. Sexual Behavior in the Human Female.
Philadelphia: Saunders, 1953.

Kirdendall, Lester A. Sex Education as Human Relations. New
York: Inor, 1950.

Maslow, A. H. (Editor) New Knowledge in Human Values. New York:
Harper, 1959.

McGary, J. L. Human Sexuality. New York: Van Nostrand
Reinhold, 2nd edition, 1973.

Ploscowe, Morris. Sex and the Law. New York: Prentice-Hall,
1951.

Schmalhausen, Samuel D. "Family Life: A Study in Pathology," pp.
275-303, in Calverton, V. F. & Schmalhausen, S. D. (Editors) The New
Generation. New York: Macaulay, 1930.

Sears, Robert. Survey of Objective Studies of Psychoanalytic
Concepts. New York: Social Science Research Council, 1947.

Vincent, Clark E. "The Cost of Naivete in Sex Education," pp. 15-23, in
Farber, Seymour M. & Wilson, Roger H. L. (Editors) Sex Education & the
Teenager. Berkeley: Diablo Press, 1967.

"American youth are continually being extended both privileges and responsibilities which recognize their increased knowledge and social autonomy as compared to their parents' and grandparents' generations. Youth have been taught to ask questions, to search for answers based on evidence, to test solutions, and to seek new ones if the first ones do not work. We approve this state of mind in most areas, but are distressed with it when it comes to sex."

Lester A. Kirkendall

(in Ard & Ard, 1976, p. 307)

CHAPTER 4
ADOLESCENTS AND SEX

Adolescents may face the most troublesome problems regarding sex because with the onset of puberty sexual interests, sexual desires and the problems associated with sex (i.e., what to do about it) are forced on them more urgently and yet conventional society provides no acceptable outlet for them. Adolescents are expected, under the conventional morality, to put off doing anything about sex for many years, until they ultimately can find at that time their "one and only" and enter into a lifelong, monogamous marriage. Sex can only then enter their life, according to the conventional plan.

Adolescents in our culture typically have many problems with sex during the period when they are becoming physiologically mature. Problems with their changing body image and all that entails, problems with dating, going steady, petting, getting emotionally involved with the first members of the other sex, masturbation, concerns with masculinity and femininity, and all in all, what to do about sex, premaritally or maritally, are some of the ethical dilemmas that adolescents typically face in this culture with many conflicting ideas and feelings as well as many moral assumptions and unquestioned premises about sex.

Body Image

Concerns about sexual matters obviously enter into adolescents' minds long before the possibility of marriage is a realistic option. With the advent of puberty and the arrival of secondary sexual characteristics, adolescents frequently begin to worry about their sexuality, their masculinity or their femininity and their sexual future. Body image is a problem for many adolescents since few measure up to what they consider adequate standards despite the fact that few are beautiful or handsome, they practically all eventually develop "standard equipment" which will enable them to function adequately sexually if they can overcome the self-defeating nature of what the conventional culture teaches them either explicitly or implicitly in the churches, the homes and the mass media.

Girls are often very much concerned about their breast development and boys about the size of their penis. (Ard, 1974, pp. 15-26) Acne and "good looks" are usually of concern to many in both sexes. Girls (and boys) need to know about menstruation (Ard, 1974, pp. 29-40) and other matters pertaining to psycho-sexual development. (Pomeroy, 1968, 1969) Boys and girls, before adolescence, need to know about such matters as pubic hair, voice changes, nocturnal emissions (or "wet dreams"), endocrine changes and their effects, and what is normal sexual development. All young people do not grow and develop at the same rate. "Late bloomers" need to know that they are just as worth while as those who blossom fast.

There are many misconceptions and misunderstandings about normal psychosexual development. Some of these fallacies are fostered by what even some professionals have taught. For example, human beings are not born bisexual, as some psychoanalysts and some homophiles would have us believe. Rather, human beings are multi-sexual or plurisexual animals. (Albert Ellis, 1965, p. 201) The concept of "bisexuality" is related to the psychoanalytic speculation about "latent homosexuality," i.e., that there is a normal stage of development in all individuals during which everyone has a problem with their "latent homosexuality." This concept has little scientific evidence to support it, like the concept of "latency period," which psychoanalysts presume is a period between early childhood and puberty when every child is supposed to be not very interested in sex. Adolescents would be a lot less bothered about the sexual problems of growing up if they could be taught the scientific data which is relevant here, rather than these psychoanalytic assumptions and speculations.

This concept of bisexuality is a myth and can no longer be accepted as fact. As Salzman (1970, p. 203) has noted, the concept of bisexuality is strongly disputed by most biologists and its application to humans is highly doubtful. However, the myth that every individual has both heterosexual and homosexual traits dies very slowly, unfortunately. Adolescents are troubled by assumptions that lead them to wonder if they are homosexual when they are growing through adolescence. Scientific knowledge at this time would help adolescents have less doubts about themselves as human beings.

A lot of common assumptions in our culture about "blondeness" cause many adolescent girls too much unnecessary concern. The psychiatrist Roderic Gorney has spelled out many of the unfortunate ramifications of these and related concepts in his book The Human Agenda (1972, pp. 506-552)

Dating

Because of the rating and dating complex, with all that the dating game implies, many adolescents have a very rough time when they begin dating. Because rating one's self can cause all sorts of self-defeating results, adolescents had better learn to distinguish between their intrinsic and their extrinsic worth whileness as persons, no matter how many, or how few, dates they have.

If one has many dates, and is therefore "popular," then on must be "attractive" and loveable, is the way this reasoning goes. Some parents even push their children into early dating for the vicarious enjoyment but to the detriment of the adolescent where the "popularity" does not prove sufficient to the parents.

Dating has many implications for masculinity and femininity and one's sexual attractiveness. Many adolescents retreat into "going steady" too soon to avoid the seeming (to them) threats to their self-esteem in risking the possibility of rejection in dating a variety of people ("playing the field"). A more rational approach would be to learn, by practicing, that one need not be overwhelmed by rejection. One can practice asking many people for dates and learn not to catastrophize over other people having the right to say "No, thanks." (Even if they omit the "thanks," they do have the right to say no.)

Petting

Getting the date for many adolescents is only the beginning of their problems in this area, only "getting to first base," so to speak. Perhaps petting is getting to second base, etc., and "scoring" means having sexual intercourse. But before the adolescents even get to sexual intercourse, they frequently have many problems with petting. Petting is problem for many adolescents because not everyone agrees as to what the proper limits are with regard to these matters.

There are many questions involved around petting in this culture. Will petting help or harm future marital adjustment, specifically sexual adjustment in marriage? Who should initiate petting? How does one know how for to go?

There are many people who still feel today that any petting before marriage is wrong and sinful. But an increasing number of people these days are taking a more liberal view with regard to petting. This in itself poses a problem for adolescents because adolescents frequently never discuss such matters across the sex lines in the battle between the sexes; they usually just get into wrestling matches (groping around in the dark) with many hurt feelings because the other person does not respond to the non-verbal cues the way one had hoped. There are few good mind readers these days it would seem.

Petting here may be taken to mean any caressing or fondling of a girl or boy (usually below the neck), with the intent of sexual arousal or satisfaction. Now obviously a girl can take the initiative and "pet" a boy, too (and many liberated females do), but the initiative is traditionally thought of as belonging to the male in this regard. Sometimes it is assumed that the boy should try to get as far as he can, while the girl is supposed to set the limits. Such assumptions are clearly irrational on several counts. More rational assumptions, and better ethics, would be to assume that each partner is responsible for their actions, can take the initiative on occasion, discuss the limits they mutually want, and are prepared to consider all the probable consequences to the various alternative courses of action.

But adolescents rarely talk out their views about petting beforehand with the other sex. Blind groping rather than rational discussion seems to be the preferred mode of interaction with regard to petting among adolescents.

Petting as a prelude to sexual intercourse is normal and natural and causes no harm in and of itself. However, if adolescents develop a pattern of premarital petting which always stops short of orgasm, this can lead to unfortunate consequences for both sexes. Petting which is never continued to orgasm can be very frustrating to both male and females and may result in unpleasant states of tension, pains in the groin or testicular region, headaches and other signs of physical and psychological discomfort. Prolonged petting without ever getting any release through orgasm may result in pelvic congestion which might lead to ailments of the genital tract, according to some authorities. (Ard, Treating Psychosexual Dysfunction, 1974, p. 4)

Some adolescents pet to orgasm frequently but always avoid sexual intercourse at all costs. When petting is practiced exclusively as a means of achieving orgasm (with sexual intercourse avoided at all costs), it may prove to be a form of sexual compulsiveness. But petting as a prelude to sexual intercourse can be most helpful.

If more young men practiced a wide variety of petting techniques, it might help out later on in their marriages. Particularly if a young man has petted with a variety of women and has learned that a variety of techniques are necessary to stimulate and satisfy different women, he will be in a better position to help his wife achieve orgasm. And if young women learn to accept and enjoy someone fondling and caressing various parts of their body, they will probably have a better sexual adjustment in marriage.

Thus petting which is openly and honestly arrived at can serve as an excellent learning experience. It can help people learn about their own bodily responses, how to let themselves go, how to relax, what they particularly enjoy, what excites them and brings sexual satisfaction. Some practical experience in petting can serve to make both males and females more knowledgeable and thoughtful lovers and thus contribute to their sexual enjoyment as well as to their pleasure in giving and receiving love and affection.

Masturbation

Among adolescents, one of the most pressing problems is that of masturbation. Many adolescents continue to feel guilty about masturbation because of what the conventional sex morality teaches about masturbation, i.e., that it is sinful, evil, self-abuse, an affront to God, a mis-use of the body, etc. Adolescents need the scientific facts clearly presented in their sex education in the schools if they are going to use these facts to overcome the faulty indoctrination they have received about sex from the traditional, conventional sex morality. Adolescents need to know that scientific evidence clearly indicates that masturbation is a normal, expected, natural phenomenon in our culture.

> *"If we, in our society, seem to have a section of people who are irredeemably crude in their sex lives, it is because we have made them so, through the inhibited attitudes still prevalent in society. These are passed on to young people as unnecessary guilt and shame about sex with all the ugly consequences." (James Hemming, Individual Morality, 1969, pp. 129-130)*

If adolescents would base their attitudes on masturbation on data rather than dogma, that is scientific evidence rather than the suppositions of supernatural religious dogma, they would be more rational and also, probably, much happier. Many recent books on sex have not been quite so hard on masturbation as previous books, but unfortunately have talked about masturbation as dangerous "if carried to excess," whatever that might mean. This fear of "excessive" masturbation is simply unjustified because the body has a natural, built-in means to prevent such so-called excess. Tumescence, or the filling of the blood vessels of the penis, for example, which is necessary for masturbation in males, will simply not occur when a person's physiological limits are approached. (Ard, Treating Psychosexual Dysfunction, 1974, pp. 44-45) But a lot of the old anti-sex attitudes still prevail in many sex manuals of today.

> "Altogether, then, the weasel-worded attitudes on masturbation which still fill most of our sex manuals, attitudes which state or imply that autoeroticism, while not completely harmful, is still not 'good' or 'desirable,' have no scientific foundation and constitute a modern carry-over of old antisexual moralizings." (Albert Ellis, 1958, p. 25)

If good sex education could be provided in the public schools, colleges and universities, then adolescents could learn that scientific evidence clearly shows that masturbation is not harmful. In fact,

> "It is difficult to conceive of a more beneficial, harmless, tension-releasing human act than masturbation that is spontaneously performed without (puritanically-inculcated and actually groundless) fears and anxieties." (Albert Ellis, 1958, p. 25)

Adolescents may want to consult professional help if they continue to feel guilty and miserable about masturbation. Some of the old teachings are sometimes hard to overcome for those indoctrinated with the old traditional, conventional morality. But one does not have to continue to feel guilty about a perfectly natural, normal act such as masturbation. Competent counselors who are rational in their orientation can be of real help to adolescents in this regard.

Premarital Coitus Among Adolescents

Of course the problem that probably receives the most concern and attention among the older generation is whether or not adolescents are committing "the act" (i.e., premarital intercourse). Sex in the form of "the act" greatly concerns many parents with regard to their adolescents (and for some parents, any adolescents). Premarital intercourse is of sufficient importance to receive fuller and separate treatment in the following chapter where it is of concern to everyone of all age ranges, but with regard to adolescents, a few points had better be clarified here.

Conventional sex morality, in its wholesale condemnation of sex, provides neither parents nor adolescents with many rational alternatives. But rational sex ethics would surely include the possibility at least of helping adolescents to learn to make more rational choices and decisions, to learn to discriminate appropriately, to consider probable consequences (long-term as well as short-term), and how to integrate sex into their lives in a meaningful, responsible way. As the psychotherapist Robert A. Harper has put it,

> "... it would be desirable to educate young people
> frankly in how to use sex as an important part of their
> skills in interpersonal relations. The suggestion here made
> is not only to stop teaching them that premarital sexual

intercourse is bad, but to teach them how to exercise their own critical faculties about deciding under what sorts of circumstances and with what sorts of partners it is likely to be functionally desirable for all parties concerned. ... The writer would trust young people, thus educated, to have considerably superior judgment in such matters to the second-hand judgments that come to them from ready-made codes of moralists." (Harper, in Ard & Ard, 1976, p. 55)

Conventional adults frequently convey to young people the idea that it is all right, so to speak, to "hang your clothes on a hickory limb, but don't go near the water," as far as sex is concerned. (Ard, in Farber & Wilson, 1967a, p. 80) As a result of this overemphasis on preventing any premarital sex at all costs among adolescents, we get increasing homosexuality and young people who sometimes seem to feel that "anything goes" just as long as they do not have premarital intercourse. So some young people will indulge in any and all sex acts (except premarital intercourse) and think they are still "technical virgins," as some young women have put it.

Puberty is coming earlier to our young people, and the education needed to prepare them for adequate functioning in our complex, technologically advanced society takes an increasingly longer time, compared to previous generations. Therefore it would seem that we had better come to some new conclusions regarding sex; our previous moralistic assumptions will simply not satisfy our young people of today who are learning to think critically. Simply turning to earlier marriage is merely avoiding the real issues as well as bringing about more problems (Ard, in Farber & Wilson, 1967b), which will always be with us until we get at the root of our culture's sexual problems: that is, our moralistic assumptions about sex.

The sociologist Ira Reiss has pointed out that our young people have been assuming more responsibility for their own sexual standards and behavior. (Reiss, in Ard & Ard, 1969, p. 255) The influence of their parents has been progressively declining. Reiss has reported on about 1,200 high school and college students, 16 to 22 years old, from three different states. (Reiss, in Ard & Ard, 1969, p. 255) He found 64 percent of those who consider coitus acceptable are actually having coitus; only 7 percent of those who accept nothing beyond petting, and 4 percent of those who accept nothing beyond kissing, are having coitus. (Reiss, in Ard & Ard, 1969, p. 257)

What can we conclude about adolescents and sex? That astute observer of the social scene, Lawrence K. Frank, has said in his book The Conduct of Sex, that

"When young people talk about their major concern, their hopes, and aspirations, and reveal their evaluations, one soon discovers that they are not only critical of their parents but they are urgently seeking some guides, some ethics for their sex interests and functions. But they can find little or no help in the search for sex ethics since very little has been done to try to formulate even the basic questions of a sex ethics." (Frank, 1961, p. 148)

This present book, in its entirety, is an attempt to formulate just what Frank says is lacking. However, such an attempt is bound to run into criticism. As Frank has noted,

"Until recently, anyone who dared to question

traditional sex morality invited vehement attacks and often prosecution as an enemy of society, as one who was subverting social order and trying to undermine religion. Today, however, we are faced not with theories and abstraction but with cumulating evidence of what our sex morals are doing to human lives and to social order.

We are beginning to realize that, as our traditional sex morality loses its customary control, we are faced with the lack of an adequate sex ethics by which individuals, especially young men and women, can guide their lives and use their sexual capacities for the fulfillment that men and women have long sought but have rarely attained." (Frank, The Conduct of Sex, 1961, pp. 136-137)

CHAPTER 4 REFERENCES

Ard, Ben. "Do As I Do, Be As I Am: The Bruising Conflict,"
pp. 78-88 in Farber, Seymour M. & Wilson, Roger H. L. (Editors) Sex
Education & The Teenager. Berkeley: Diablo Press, 1967a.

Ard, Ben. "Gray Hair for the Teen-age Father," pp. 95-104, in
Farber, Seymour M. & Wilson, Roger h. L. (Editors) Teenage Marriage &
Divorce. Berkeley: Diablo Press, 1967b.

Ard, Ben N., Jr. Treating Psychosexual Dysfunction. New York:
Jason Aronson, 1974.

Ellis, Albert. "Thoughts on Petting," pp. 26-32, in Ellis,
Albert. Sex Without Guilt. New York: Lyle Stuart, 1958.

Ellis, Albert. "New Light on Masturbation," pp. 15-25, in Ellis,
Albert. Sex Without Guilt. New York: Lyle Stuart, 1958.

Gorney, Roderic. The Human Agenda. New York: Simon & Schuster,
1972.

Harper, Robert A. "Moral Issues in Marital Counseling," pp. 48-
57, in Ard, Ben N., Jr. & Ard, C. C. (Editors) Handbook of Marriage
Counseling. Palo Alto: Science & Behavior Books, 2nd edition, 1976.

Hemming, James. Individual Morality. London: Panther Modern
Society, 1970.

Kirkendall, Lester A. "A Counselor Looks at Contraceptives for
the Unmarried," pp. 303-317, in Ard, Ben N. Jr. & Ard C. C. (Editors)
Handbook of Marriage Counseling. Palo Alto: Science & Behavior Books,
2nd edition, 1976.

Pomeroy, Wardell B. Boys and Sex. New York: Delacorte Press,
1968.

Pomeroy, Wardell B. Girls and Sex. New York: Delacorte Press, 1969.

Pomeroy, Wardell B. <u>Girls and Sex</u>. New York: Delacorte Press, 1969.

Reiss, Ira L. "How and Why America's Sex Standards Are Changing," pp. 255-263, in Ard, Ben N., Jr. & Ard, C. C. (Editors) <u>Handbook of Marriage Counseling</u>. Palo Alto: Science & Behavior Books, 1969.

"These pre-marital relations entered into between socially equal individuals on grounds of personal love cannot be summarily condemned for ethical reasons, according to the opinion of the Commission. Under the circumstances this is from ethical, and definitely from hygienic and social viewpoints, a better solution of a complicated human problem than was the old double standard."

A. Myrdal (Quoted in Atkinson, 1965, p. 99)

CHAPTER 5
PREMARITAL SEX

Premarital sex has probably been one of the crucial issues regarding sex for a long time. Obviously as we shall see elsewhere in this book there are lots of ethical dilemmas on a wide ranging plethora of problems having to do with sex. But many people, when asked what the primary problem with regard to sex is, specifically, probably would say "premarital sex."

It has been called "free love" on some occasions and sometimes been arbitrarily defined as "promiscuity" or even identified broadly as any and all sex outside of marriage, which is a very loose way of looking at the matter (no pun intended). The latter terminology is confusing premarital sex with extramarital sex, and some writers even use the term nonmarital sex. In this chapter we shall confine the discussion to premarital sex.

Cross-cultural Considerations

Conventional sex morality in our culture has, of course, come down most strongly against premarital sex. A lot of naive people assume that most "civilized" societies prohibit premarital sex, thus acknowledging (reluctantly) that perhaps some "wild savages" might do it. But as Morton Hunt, who has reported on one of the most recent surveys of sexual behavior, has said,

> "Western society has thus been most unusual in its proscription of premarital sexual activity. Statistically speaking, this is abnormal; and it is abnormal in the deeper sense, for the evidence amassed by

deeper sense, for the evidence amassed by
psychotherapists, marriage counselors and sociologists has
shown our society's ban on premarital sexual activity to
be productive of much needless misery and innumerable
emotional and sexual disorders and malfunctions." (Hunt,
1974, p. 111)

Rather than just casting aspersions against so-called "primitive" cultures, we need to recognize that we could learn a lot from cross-cultural studies in this regard. As Grace Stuart has pointed out,

"Social sentiments in their simplest forms of happy,
affectionate, unafraid and peaceable relationships do in
fact seem most to prevail in these 'primitive' societies
which have the least sense of sin about the sexual
function..." (Grace Stuart, 1951, p. 166)

Because some of these so-called primitive cultures have been underdeveloped countries, they have been frequently ignored by the so-called "higher" or more civilized countries. An unfortunate attitude, as Grace Stuart has said:

"there do exist, and have existed, cultures, generally
small, where sex has been treated unfearfully and non-
repressively, and where it does seem to have contributed
considerably both to race-preservation and human peace
and happiness. But many of these cultures have been too
unsophisticated and underdeveloped to show all that sex
might contribute both to the greater freedom and
happiness of men and women, and to the greater peace

and creativity of the community." (Grace Stuart, 1951, pp.
26-27)

Anthropologists can contribute to rational sex ethics by revealing in their cross-cultural studies how various cultures have handled sex in a variety of settings. We can continue to learn from other cultures, even the so-called underdeveloped and small cultures.

Deciding About Premarital Sex

Although conventional sex morality has been adamantly against premarital sex for a long time in our culture, it is time to question traditional prohibitions of all premarital sex. Many of these prohibitions are obviously out of order.

> *"in the realm of sex, perhaps more than in any other*
> *contemporary aspect of living, it is dubious that most so-*
> *called errors, wrongs, or sins are truly wrong. For by*
> *'wrong' we mean that an act needlessly harms one's self,*
> *needlessly harms another person, or both; and*
> *exceptionally few premarital sex behaviors are, in their*
> *own right, in this category." (Albert Ellis, in Grummon &*
> *Barclay, 1971, p. 229)*

How would a rational person go about deciding whether or not to indulge in premarital sex, and if so, under what circumstances and with what sorts of partners? Most people these days might think this is an odd sort of question since they may usually decide such matters on the basis of "feelings," as it is currently put.

"Feelings" have been elevated to a sacrosanct position these days in much of contemporary life. Some people seem to assume that feelings can justify just about any behavior, sexual or otherwise. The answer to just about any behavior, if one asks why the person did it, is likely to be "Because I felt like it," as if that were sufficient explanation.

> "*similarly, some believe that if one performs under the influence of a feeling, one's behavior is excusable, as well as explainable. What is especially implausible about views of this sort is that no analysis has as yet been made of feeling that shows it to be of a higher value than any other psychological entity; nor has any analysis been made that shows that behavior caused by feeling has any comparatively privileged position that makes it immune from praise or blame. Of course one might argue that behavior caused by feeling is uncontrollable; but why should that fact, if indeed it is one, make such behavior more valuable than merely rational or calculative or habitual behavior." (Baumrin, in Baker & Elliston, 1975, p. 122)*

Other concepts had better be brought into the discussion of premarital sexual relationships are to be more rationally entered into, it would seem. A concept that may lie at the heart of sexual relationships is the mutual consent principle of contemporary jurisprudence. As stated by one authority (Holmes, 1972, p. 714), "People may do what they wish with each other if all concerned are in agreement, and if their conduct does not encroach unduly upon the equivalent rights of others."

> "*Ideally, the mutual consent principle carries over to*

the everyday negotiations of people in their interpersonal relationships. Each person grants every other person first rights to his own being, to his body, his life. Its application at this level insists upon an easy and immediate right to freedom of choice, either to proceed or to disengage and withdraw, at any stage of an ongoing relationship. All parties concerned would hold themselves obligated to honor this right, without force, threats, derision, or embarrassing entreaties, no matter how intense their own state of arousal." (Homes, 1972, p. 714)

If we are going to follow scientific evidence in coming to more rational sex conclusions, then we will be forced to come to different value judgments than heretofore reached by conventional moralists about premarital sex. As the psychologist Dr. Albert Ellis has stated,

"Some research evidence (Kinsey, et al, 1948, 1953) and considerable clinical data indicate that modern couples who try sex, particularly with each other, before marriage tend to have better sex lives after mating and are less prone to corrosive disillusionment than those who enter the marital state in complete sexual ignorance." (Albert Ellis, in Grummon & Barclay, 1971, p. 230)

If premarital sex is to be viewed, under rational sex ethics, as a legitimate endeavor under certain circumstances, people had better learn to handle overtures and rejections regarding premarital sex. At least all such overtures, for example, cannot rationally be interpreted as an insulting proposition. As a psychiatrist, Donald J. Homes, has so delightfully put it:

"There is also much to be gained by learning to distinguish between a courteous invitation and an indecent proposition. Another person's considerately expressed interest in you is not an insult, but a compliment. If you are not interested, decline politely with a 'thank you all the same.' If he persists and wheedles, give him exit instructions politely but firmly." (Holmes, 1972, p. 714)

Helping people handle premarital sexual relationships in a more rational manner would seem to be a better approach than the traditional condemnations of conventional moralists.

"The frequent suggestion that young people who have premarital sexual relationships are morally inferior to chaste ones is not supported by the evidence. What is important is not whether or not sexual relationships take place, but the quality of the relationships." (James Hemming, 1969, p. 137) [Cf., also, L. A. Kirkendall, 1961]

The argument against premarital sex by traditionalists have frequently in the past railed strongest against what has been called "free love." Let us look at this matter from a logical point of view.

Free Love

It has been a traditionalist argument against premarital sex, or free love, that such affairs before marriage will make people more ready to engage in adulterous affairs after marriage, and consequently threaten the stability and durability of marriage. (Atkinson, 1965, p. 77) However, empirical research evidence (Ard, 1974a) does not support such a point of view or show that this is the case in marriages followed over twenty years.

Humanly speaking, free love or premarital sex is going to occur. As Atkinson has put it, "It has in any event to be recognized that premarital intercourse cannot be argued out of existence." (Atkinson, 1965, p. 101) A more rational approach would help people make wiser choices rather than arbitrarily condemning themselves and others for very human, understandable behavior. Bertrand Russell, the famous British philosopher, in his book Marriage and Morals (1929), has stated that "To secure as little interference with love as is compatible with the interests of children should be one of the main purposes of a wise sexual ethic." (Russell, 1929, pp. 66-67) The implications of this position of Russell's are clear: where there are no children, love should be entirely free. Thus premarital sex would be entirely acceptable under certain circumstances.

However, "free love" is a somewhat misleading expression, as the philosopher Frederick Elliston has pointed out: "...like everything else, sex has its price assessed in terms of time, effort, emotional tensions, and a trade off of other benefits and burdens." (Elliston, in Baker & Elliston, 1975, p. 225) In fact, Elliston has met another traditional argument in this area head on and come out with an excellent discussion in defense of "promiscuity," another term that is easily bandied about in many discussions of premarital sex by conventional moralists.

Promiscuity

"Promiscuity" has been the arbitrary label hung on all premarital sex by many traditional moralists. Yet, obviously, if promiscuity is taken to mean indiscriminate premarital intercourse, the supposedly opposite extreme from monogamy (or the monogamous marriage in the conventional view), it is misnomer, since some people may have one premarital affair that lasts practically a lifetime, yet may be quite monogamous within that relationship. Some people may be very discriminating in choosing what partners (who may be very few in number) that they will have premarital sex with; that can hardly be said to be promiscuity in any realistic and logical sense.

But let us look at this whole matter of "promiscuity" with the logical acuity of the philosopher Frederick Elliston. (Elliston, in Baker & Elliston, 1974, pp. 222-243) He has clearly pointed out that it is logically false to say that a promiscuous person is necessarily indiscriminate and too facile to try to assess promiscuity merely in terms of numbers. (Elliston, in Baker & Elliston, 1975, p. 224)

Promiscuity, as Elliston uses the concept, means sex with a series of other adults, not directly related through marriage, with no commitments. (Elliston, in Baker & Elliston, 1975, p. 225) As he has stated:

> *"Promiscuity asserts a freedom from the obligation within or without marriage to 'love, honor and obey' and a freedom to engage in sex with any peer who agrees. These refusals to issue promissory notes for affection and support throughout an indefinite future and to issue a guarantee of sexual exclusivity are promiscuity's most significant departure from the traditional sexual norm."*
> *(Elliston, in Baker & Elliston, 1975, p. 226)*

As Elliston clearly and logically shows, promiscuity cannot be shown to be wrong in all cases and does not necessarily have to be exploitative, as some traditionalists have tried to argue. Elliston, therefore, comes to a more rational conclusion about promiscuity:

> *"When the threat of pregnancy is minimized, sex for*

*its own sake becomes possible, enjoyable, and desirable
thereby making many of the earlier reasons for lying,
deceiving, and exploiting invalid. That promiscuity must
involve immoral behavior then becomes an anachronism, an
empirical claim that is no longer true. Promiscuity per se
or prima facie is not wrong." (Elliston, in Baker &
Elliston, 1974, p. 230)*

While we have tried to avoid any simple use of the words "good" and
"bad," sometimes it still seems clearest to make the point in a
straightforward manner, as Elliston has: "Insofar as promiscuity maximizes
the pleasures that can be derived from sex, it is good; and insofar as the
prohibition against promiscuity is a limitation on the pleasures to be derived
from sex, it is unwarranted -- in a word, 'bad.'" (Elliston, in Baker &
Elliston, 1975, p. 233) Some people have objected to premarital sex for the
reason that there is a lack of commitment to marriage. But as Elliston has
stated, "The lack of commitment that characterizes promiscuity is a freedom
to explore patterns of sexual behavior at variance with the tradition. This
exploration can engage one's 'higher faculties' of reason, judgment, and good
taste." (Elliston, in Baker & Elliston, 1975, p. 234)

Premarital Sex Tomorrow

So ultimately the problem of premarital sex reduces to what one's basic
attitude toward sex is. If one arbitrarily defines sex as bad outside of
marriage (that is, a sin, according to the conventional sex morality) then
one may indeed have a problem. (Ard, 1974b, pp. 56-67) However, if one
wishes to follow a more rational sex ethics and think of sex as a normal,
natural, good part of life, when handled with reason, discretion,

accountability, and good taste, then premarital sex can be integrated into a good life, despite the fact that many people in our culture continue to have many irrational ideas and assumptions about premarital sex.

As Albert Ellis has put it,

> "...almost all groups and individuals now advocating wider premarital freedom want man's so-called sex instincts to be solidly embedded in a context of honesty, consideration, mutual consent, and even love. What we sexual libertarians invariably fight for is the removal of arbitrary, needless, foolish, anxiety-abetting, and hostility-fermenting fetters on sex relations. Of course we do not want complete sex freedom any more than we want removal of all restrictions on business transactions, on automobile driving, or on using weapons." (Albert Ellis, in Grummon & Barclay, 1971, p. 233)

If premarital sex is to be a viable, rational choice for people tomorrow, however, certain prior decisions about reliable birth control methods and "safer" sex need to be made. To these issues we shall turn in the next chapter.

CHAPTER 5 REFERENCES

Ard, Ben N., Jr. "Premarital Sexual Experience: A Longitudinal
Study," Journal of Sex Research, Vol. 10, No. 1, pp. 32-39, February,
1974a.

Ard, Ben J., Jr. "Premarital Sex," pp. 55-67, in Ard, Ben N.,
Jr. Treatment Psychosexual Dysfunction. New York: Jason Aronson,
1974b.

Atkinson, Ronald. Sexual Morality. New York: Harcourt, Brace &
World, 1965.

Baumrin, Bernard H. "Sexual Immorality Delineated," pp. 116-128,
in Baker, Robert & Elliston, Frederick (Editors) Philosophy & Sex.
Buffalo: Prometheus Books, 1975.

Ellis, Albert. "On Premarital Sex Relations," pp. 33-50, in
Ellis, Albert. Sex Without Guilt. New York: Lyle Stuart, 1958.

Ellis, Albert. "Sex Without Guilt," pp. 226-244, in Grummon,
Donald L. & Barclay, Andrew M. (Editors) Sexuality: A Search for
Perspective. New York: Van Nostrand Reinhold, 1971.

Elliston, Frederick. "In Defense of Promiscuity," pp. 222-243,
in Baker, Robert & Elliston, Frederick (Editors) Philosophy & Sex.
Buffalo: Prometheus Books, 1975.

Hemming, James. Individual Morality. London: Panther Modern
Society, 1970.

Holmes Donald J. Psychotherapy. Boston: Little, Brown, 1972. Hunt, Morton.
Sexual Behavior in the 1970's. New York: Dell,
1974.

Kirdendall, Lester A. Premarital Intercourse and Interpersonal
Relationship. New York: Julian Press, 1961.

<u>Relationship</u>. New York: Julian Press, 1961.

Russell, Bertrand. <u>Marriage and Morals</u>. London: Unwin, 1929.

Stuart, Grace. <u>Conscience and Reason</u>. New York: MacMillan, 1951.

"The passions and pleasures of sex, manifesting the intense affection of one human being for another, are blessing that ought to be supported by reason, not blemished or curtailed by the deliberate refusal to use reason. The rational control of birth requires the deliberate separation of the procreative function from the unitive function when appropriate."

Carl Cohen

(in Baker & Elliston, 1975, p. 155)

CHAPTER 6

Safer Sex in an Era of Birth Control
STDs, Herpes and AIDS

If a rational sex ethics would argue for certain conditions under which premarital and marital sex would be acceptable, would there be any different conditions under which such premarital or marital sex would <u>not</u> be a good idea? What immediately comes to mind would be those conditions under which one of the partners does not use any birth control methods, or has STDs (sexually transmitted diseases) such as, for example, herpes or AIDS.

In view of the recent epidemic nature of such diseases as herpes (for which there is, as yet, no known cure) and AIDS (which leads rather inevitably to death, at our current state of medical knowledge), people had better learn to be much more aware, more fully educated, and more carefully discriminating about who they have sex with and under what conditions. It may be said that "safe sex" is perhaps a good, brief term from the point of view of the mass media, but to be more specific, precise and scientifically accurate, there may be some good reasons for arguing that there is no <u>completely</u> "safe" sex. That is, if partners have sex where they do not know whether their partner has a sexually transmittable disease or not, or is using any reliable method of birth control or not, sex in those circumstances can hardly be considered "safe." We shall start out with perhaps the oldest concern: birth control and unwanted pregnancies.

Birth Control

For many years value judgments against birth control methods were used by a very influential religious minority group in our culture to, in effect, control the sexual behavior of the majority who did not agree with the moral premises of the religious minority. Laws were extant for many years forbidding any dissemination of information regarding birth control methods. Thus fear of pregnancy was used as a weapon in frightening many women into unnecessary ethical dilemmas regarding sex. Fear of getting a woman pregnant can trouble men, too. Fear of getting pregnant can cause a woman to have trouble with sex. Now with the pill and other new birth control methods, sex can be clearly kept separated from reproduction.

It is a sad commentary on our society that religious assumptions of a minority have prevented the widespread use of birth control methods and thus enhanced the population explosion. "For the first time in human history it is now possible to regulate conception reliably, and on the success of such regulation the future of mankind may hinge." (Katchadourian & Lunde, 1975, p. 145)

The majority of Americans are squarely behind proper instruction in birth control, and have been shown to be so in repeated surveys, over many years. But a minority, for religious reasons that the majority do not agree with, have opposed birth control and have been able to influence legislatures, schools, and colleges so that it is difficult to teach preventive methods, even today. (Ard, 1974, pp. 109-120)

The Church's Arguments

The attempts of the Roman Catholic church to prevent anyone from using birth control methods deserve vigorous logical analysis for everyone's sake.

The church's various dogma, promulgated through the popes, are based on the crucial premise that sexual intercourse and procreation are universally and indivisibly conjoined. (Cohen, in Baker & Elliston, 1975, p. 153) However, "this fundamental premise, that the unitive and procreative functions of sex are conjoined in such a way as to be totally inseparable in every case, must be gravely questioned." (Cohen, in Baker & Elliston, 1975, p. 153) As the philosopher Carl Cohen has shown, this "inseparability" premise is simply without good foundation. Secondly, it is simply false.

> *"Papal authority, however, persuasive for some*
> *Catholics, cannot constitute proof for a moderately*
> *rational man. Too often have popes proclaimed as true and*
> *binding what has later been admitted (at a time too late*
> *to remedy the injury done) to be blatantly false."*
> *(Cohen, in Baker & Elliston, 1975, p. 154)*

The whole religious frame of mind involved in Pope Paul VI's 1968 encyclical letter regarding birth control presumes that "the Church alone knows what God plans and knows exactly what instruments He has decided we may use in helping Him to accomplish these plans." (Cohen, in Baker & Elliston, 1975, p. 154) "In elevating fallible human opinions on controversial issues to the status of divine will, this encyclical, like many before it, makes a false and deceptive appeal, seeking to shield dogma from rational criticism." (Cohen, in Baker & Elliston, 1975, p. 154)

The argument of the religious that sexual intercourse might be more widely enjoyed if birth control methods were more available and used is simply intolerable. (Cohen , in Baker & Elliston, 1975, p. 163) If religious people do not wish to use birth control methods, that is their prerogative.

But they have no right to influence legislatures to pass laws to prevent non-religious people from using any rational, reasonable means to limit unwanted pregnancies.

Abortion

The church's long-standing position against therapeutic abortion has rested on several premises: (1) every human being has a soul, (2) that soul is present from the moment of conception, (3) there is a supreme "god," and (4) he is against abortion. However, as Donald J. Holmes, a psychiatrist, has stated, "...there is not and never has been the least shred of credible evidence that there is a body-specific 'soul' which has an independent existence either before birth or after death..." (Holmes, 1972, p. 637) Also, "...there is no known 'God' who has shown the least concern for the mortal fate or welfare of individual people." (Holmes, 1972, p. 637)

Traditionalists have argued that abortion equals murder. But this argument has been ably answered by Dr. Alan F. Guttmacher, who is president of Planned Parent World Population:

"I do not look upon abortion as a form of murder. To me, there is no similarity between the rights of an adult individual and her family compared with embryonic cells that have not yet become a human being, that are laid down according to the pattern of a human being but have had as yet no human experience and are still incapable of thought. This is not murder. This is simply, in my point of view, the value of the adult life against a group of embryonic cells that have the potentiality of becoming a human being. You may say this is splitting

hairs, this is semantics; to me it is not." (Guttmacher, in
Grummon & Barclay, 1971, p. 183)

The consequences for many people who get pregnant are sometimes so depleting (after too many children) that they understandably withdraw from any further sex contacts. Or they may feel so guilty about considering birth control or abortion that they are unable to think straight about the ethical issues involved. This is particularly likely to be the case of their moral upbringing has led them to believe that birth control and/or abortion are sinful and affronts against God.

Bernard Goldstein has shown that psychological conflict and lack of proper motivation can lead to more contraceptive failures than chemical and/or mechanical defects of the birth control method combined. (Goldstein, 1976, p. 179)

"People who show a capacity to plan ahead, who feel
they have control over their own futures, and who feel
morally free to enjoy sexual intercourse for purposes
other than procreation have been suggested as patients
most likely to show success in family planning."
(Goldstein, 1976, p. 179)

If we have always had, and will continue to have, nonmarital sexual intercourse, as Kirkendall states (Kirkendall, in Ard & Ard, 1976, p. 304), then birth control methods, including therapeutic abortion as a back-up technique, had better be a part of any rational approach to sex. We had better get away from traditional moral approaches to these areas of birth control and abortion. As Kirkendall has concluded:

"...our traditional concepts concerning morals baffle

and impede all our efforts to arrive at more rational and
constructive ways of dealing with human sexuality."
(Kirkendall, in Ard & Ard, 1976, p. 304)

Rational people will be accountable for their sex acts and take proper responsibility for using birth control methods. If an unwanted pregnancy should happen to occur, then abortion as a rational alternative can reasonable be considered.

Romantic notions of love may have to be eliminated before people will be willing to discuss what methods of birth control they are going to use and under what circumstances they would be willing to turn to abortion, if necessary. Romantic notions of love and being swept away by passion seem to relieve some people of any notions of accountability or responsibility or planning ahead. But rational people will want to know what each other's notions about love and possible pregnancies are, along with what means they are willing to take so that no unwanted pregnancies occur or unwanted children come along when and where they cannot be properly cared for financially and emotionally. Children are not simply little angels that God sends trooping down from heaven; they are the result of having sex without taking any precautions and refusing to do anything about it when discovering an unwanted pernancy. Getting married simply when one discovers an unwanted pregnancy is frequently not a very rational decision either. And using a premarital pregnancy as a device to trap someone into marriage is hardly rational sex ethics. Honesty would seem to be particularly indicated in sexual encounters these days, what with the increasing epidemic proportions of sexually transmitted diseases.

STDs, Herpes and AIDS

For many years, before the advent of "the Pill," the threat of unwanted pregnancies was perhaps the outstanding threat to look out for as a consequence of sexual intercourse. With the development of the birth control pill, rational women could plan for their families and space their children, to the benefit of the children, the family and the woman.

Sexually transmitted diseases (STDs) have long been a possible troublesome consequence of sexual intercourse, also. Syphilis, gonorrhea, chlamydia and papillomavirus (a virus that causes growths called condylomas or genital warts) have been STDs for a long time. But the virus-caused genital herpes and AIDS (acquired immune deficiency syndrome) in recent epidemic proportions are two of the more recent and dangerous sexually transmitted diseases. Unfortunately, at the present state of medical knowledge, there is no cure for genital herpes (therefore, once infected with genital herpes, you are infected for life) and, as is well known these days, AIDS has a fatal outcome.

Does the fact that AIDS is spreading in epidemic proportions affect sexual interactions among heterosexuals as well as homosexuals? It would seem so. Just take kissing, for example. Teenagers have written to Beth Winship (a newspaper columnist who writes "Ask Beth" in the San Francisco Chronicle, Sunday Punch, Sept. 27, 1987, p. 4), asking about whether AIDS can be transmitted by kissing. Beth said: "There has been no known case of AIDS being transmitted through kissing." However, she went on to say: "Since small amounts of the AIDS virus are found in saliva, doctors feel it isn't safe to say categorically, 'No one can get AIDS through kissing.'" She added that some experts caution people not to indulge in deep, wet, so-called French kissing.

So for people wanting to be more rational about their sex ethics, added considerations would seem to be indicated since, to put it colloquially, "when you sleep with someone, you are also sleeping with everyone that person has ever slept with." That may be putting the matter somewhat crudely, but it does point out that if one partner in a sexual encounter is healthy and monogamous, while the other partner is not monogamous, and possibly bisexual, then there is the obvious possible danger of STDs to be calculated.

Rational sex ethics would seem to involve honesty about one's health and whether or not one is sleeping around (non-monogamously, and with what sorts of partners). Taking proper precautions rationally would not eliminate all risks (hence the thought that there probably cannot be any completely safe sex), but you can make sex much safer if one is willing to think ahead and plan for safer sex.

Instead of making traditional, religious (supernatural) assumptions about morality (for example, authoritarian views such as that STDs are God's way of punishing homosexuals and heterosexuals for breaking God's laws about sex), rational sex ethics would want to take a more authoritative scientific view of what facts are needed in order to make more rational decisions with regard to STDs and sex.

The scientific facts in these matters have been outlined by the American College Health Association in a pamphlet (Making Sex Safer, 1987). Summarizing some of the points they make, briefly, we may say, as they do, that "you don't have to sleep with a lot of people to get an STD, but your chances of getting something increase when you have unprotected sex with multiple partners."

The best, rational, scientific advice from the ACHA is to

"Talk about safe sex with your partner.

Ask about your partner's health and sexual history.

Be honest about your own history so that you both can

make informed decisions."

What precautions had better be taken? Again, the ACHA suggests:

"Agree to have only safe sex.

Don't engage in any high risk activities.

Use condoms to prevent exchange of body fluids."

It may be helpful, according to the ACHA, to classify kinds of activities related to sex into several categories: "Safe," "Less Risky," "Risky" and "Dangerous," as well as some comments on drugs and sex and what is "Harmful to Your Judgment."

Some of the ACHA suggestions:

SAFE

Dry kissing.

Masturbation on Healthy Skin.

LESS RISKY

Vaginal Intercourse With a Condom.

Wet kissing.

Anal Intercourse With a Condom.

RISKY

Oral Sex Without a Condom.

DANGEROUS

Vaginal Intercourse Without a Condom.

Anal Intercourse Without a Condom.

Sharing a Needle.

Fisting.

Oral-Anal Contact.

HARMFUL TO YOUR JUDGMENT

Amphetamines (speed)

Amyl Nitrite (poppers)

Alcohol

Marijuana

Cocaine

Thus we see from the ACHA that "playing safe about sex does not mean eliminating sex from your life." However, "it does mean being smart and staying healthy." That is, it means "knowing how to protect yourself and taking precautions consistently every time." Thus, we see that "playing safe means enjoying sex without giving or getting sexually transmitted diseases."

CHAPTER 6 REFERENCES

American College Health Association. Making Sex Safer.
(Pamphlet) Rockville, Maryland: American College Health Association,
1987.

Ard, Ben N., Jr. "Birth Control," pp 109-120, in Ard, Ben N., Jr.
Treating Psychosexual Dysfunction. New York: Jason Aronson, 1974.

Cohen, Carl. "Sex, Birth Control, and Human Life," pp. 150-165,
in Baker, Robert & Elliston, Frederick (Editors) Philosophy & Sex.
Buffalo: Prometheus Books, 1975.

Goldstein, Bernard. Introduction to Human Sexuality. New York:
McGraw-Hill, 1976.

Guttmacher, Alan F. "Who Owns Fertility: the Church, the State,
or the Individual?", pp. 174-187, in Grummon, Donald L. & Barclay,
Andrew M. (Editors) Sexuality: A search for Perspective. New York:
Van Nostrand Reinhold, 1971.

Homes, Donald J. Psychotherapy. Boston: Little, Brown, 1972.

Katchadouran, Herant & Lunde, Donald T. Fundamentals of Human Sexuality.
New york: Holt, Rinehart & Winston, 2nd edition, 1975.

Kirkendall, Lester A. "A Counselor Looks at Contraceptives for
the Unmarried," pp. 303-317, in Ard, Ben n., Jr. & Ard, C. C. (Editors)
Handbook of Marriage Counseling. Palo Alto: Science & Behavior
Books, 2nd edition, 1976.

"Where there is mutual freedom and no pecuniary motive, love is good; where these conditions fail, it may often be bad. It is because they fail so frequently in the conventional marriage that a morality which is positive rather than restrictive, based upon hope rather than fear, is compelled, if it is logical, to disagree with the received code in matters of sex."

Bertrand Russell

(Quoted in Wile, 1934, p. 233)

CHAPTER 7
SEX AND MARRIAGE

What factors influence the selection of marital partners? Hudson and Henze, in their research on mate selection, have stated that the choice of a mate is limited by the individual's formation of generalized value systems before maturation. (Hudson & Henze, in Wiseman, 1971, p. 73) "Whether consciously or unconsciously, the person's value system serves as criteria for mate selection." (Hudson & Henze, in Wiseman, 1971, p. 74)

As that astute observer of the social scene Max Lerner has said in his book America as a Civilization:

> "There are no people in the world who make greater demands upon marriage than Americans do, since they lay greater expectations upon it and also expect greater psychic satisfactions from it. They do not make the necessarily right demands, but whether right or wrong, they don't settle easily for a small fraction." (Lerner, 1957, p. 595)

Human sexual behavior in marriage, as Ehrmann has noted, is controlled, patterned, and channeled by customs, and this behavior is greatly influenced by symbolic thought and by the contemplation and evaluation of each person's own ideas and actions. (Ehrmann, in Christensen, 1964, p. 588) Attitudes are more important than anatomy, it would seem.

In marriage sex may continue to be a perennial problem despite the fact that, from the traditional point of view, sex is at least now legal. Some people with romantic notions and great expectations are frequently soon disappointed and disillusioned. (Ard, in Ard & Ard, 1976, pp. 286-295) As the philosopher Schopenhauer has said,

> *"Happy marriages are well known to be rare; just*
> *because it lies in the nature of marriage that its chief*
> *end is not the present but the coming generation.*
> *However, let me add, for the consolation of tender, loving*
> *natures, that sometimes passionate sexual love associates*
> *itself with a feeling of an entirely different origin -- real*
> *friendship based upon agreement of disposition, which yet*
> *for the most part only appears when sexual love proper*
> *is extinguished in its satisfaction." (Schopenhauer, quoted*
> *in Baker & Elliston, 1975, p. 13)*

However, some recent social scientists have stated that all aspects of the marital relationship are affected by its sexual aspects. (Gagnon, 1977, p. 191) The conventional morality limits sex to married people thus, in effect, forbidding any sex to those who are not married.

> *"The sex lives of those who remain single, or who*
> *are divorced or widowed, are affected by the availability*
> *of potential sexual and marital partners limited by the*
> *fact that so many people are married in the U.S.*
> *society." (Gagnon, 1977, p. 191)*

What is the quality of sex in marriage? Marital sex occurs with a relative frequency that lessens even more with age, and as Gagnon has stated, "all around us is a constant outcry about the quality of sex in marriage." (Gagnon, 1977, p. 191) Masters and Johnson (1966, 1970) have suggested that at least half of all marriages involve some sexual dysfunction.

In a longitudinal study of sex in marriage, the evidence suggests that for most of these marriages of 20 years duration, the sexual component continues to be an important one. (Ard, 1977) While a decrease in sexual activity occurred over time, for most of the people in these marriages there remained primarily positive feelings about sex, and satisfaction from sex. Familiarity did not breed contempt, for these couples, and novelty of partner was not necessary for continuing sexual satisfaction. (Ard, 1977)

But not everyone these days desires to view the conventional monogamous marriage as the only possibility. As the psychologist Lorine Pruette has noted:

> "A considerable number of independent and intellectual young women definitely prefer the arrangement of progressive monogamy to that of marriage, holding that they thus escape the burdens of the conventional masculine attitude toward the wife and retain a genuine advantage by the appearance of giving from desire rather than from legal fiat." (Lorine Pruette, in Wile, 1934, p. 297)

A rational code of sex ethics would certainly allow more than one alternative (i.e., conventional monogamous marriage) to members of society. In fact, by offering other possibilities, this more rational attitude toward sex ethics would probably help ease some of the tensions between the sexes.

"Sex, too, by inference from research findings and from changed social attitudes and values, seemed to become more of a positive force for solidifying male-female relations and less of an antagonistic, exploitative, and disruptive element in both premarriage and marriage."
(Ehrmann, in Christensen, 1964, pp. 595-596)

Sex and sexuality have for so long been considered in an essentially negative context that it is high time some consideration be given to the positive forces for personal and social regeneration that may be found in sex and sexuality. (Ard, in Otto, 1971, pp. 14-25) Some couples who see sex in their lives as a source of rejuvenation and revivification can see sexual encounters as an opportunity to try out all sorts of new and different approaches.

What To Do?

Probably the central question regarding sex and marriage for many people is: what sex is all right in marriage? Having been reared to think all sorts of negative things about sex, when marriage at least opens up the opportunity to have "legal" sex, what sorts of sex is acceptable? Can married people do anything?

Conventional sex morality of course severely limits what sorts of sex acts are deemed acceptable or moral. As a general principle, rational sex ethics would take the stance that a married couple are free to try any sorts of sex acts that they mutually desire, provided they have considered the consequences and the sex acts are not harmful (in the long run as well as the short run) to either or both of the people involved (as well as to any possible future offspring).

Couples had better discuss among themselves what sorts of positions, acts, and accoutrements, etc., that they would like to try and essentially adopt an open, experimental attitude which implies a certain willingness to at least try once (or perhaps a few times) some things that may seem new, or perhaps different and unusual, after having clearly checked out the probable consequences along scientific lines, not through hearsay evidence, superstition, folklore, or old wives' tales. Many books are available these days which offer many suggestions. (Ard, 1974; Comfort, 1972; Ellis, 1958, 1960, 1972; Gagnon, 1977; Harper & Stockes, 1971; Young, 1964; Zilbergeld, 1978) Every book, however, had better be read critically and thoughtfully and discussed with one's partner, rather than adopted as a bible, uncritically. Some people seem to feel as if they simply must try everything suggested in the book, as if it were a recipe book, which is patently irrational and absurd.

Each suggestion in any book had better be considered in the light of scientific knowledge available in the field, compared with other books, and weighed in terms of the possible gains versus the effort and the consequences involved. Most important of all, suggestions from such 'marriage manuals' had better be considered in terms of one' personal preferences (rather than as demands) and considering very carefully the possible consequences both negative and positive. If "everyone" is trying it because it is "kinky" or "far-out" or the "in" thing to do, that may very well be good reason to consider it very seriously and thoughtfully. (Ellis, The Sensuous Person: Critique and Corrections, 1972)

If, after trying a new position or act a few times and deciding either or both do not prefer it, there is no need to feel guilty about, for example, not enjoying sex while swinging from the chandelier. Jumping on the current bandwagon or following the fad that is popular at the moment is not necessarily being the most rational one can be.

Perhaps the sex acts that cause the most concern and sometimes difficulties in marriages are extramarital sex relations. It is common these days to see articles about 'wife-swapping' and extramarital relations in the form of 'swinging' in some of the most popular magazines.

Extramarital Relations

Many people assume that extramarital sex relations are the major cause of divorce. (Ard, 1974, pp. 145-155) Certainly many marriages have split up over the issue of extramarital relations. "Open marriages" wherein each partner is free to have extramarital relations are still very difficult for many couples in this culture, it would seem.

If we raise the question, can a person love more than one person at a time?, the answer seems to be yes, one can love more than one member of the other sex at the same time, or more accurately, during the same period of time in one's life. Perhaps the monogamous ideal which is the essence of the traditional values in our culture actually work against healthy, viable marriages. (Ard, 1972)

The monogamous ideal insists that love is "forever" and that the real thing ("true love") only comes once in a lifetime. Some even think this ideal to be a part of God's plan and any variance from it is a sin against God. Now obviously such ideas would have been relegated to the garbage heap as unrealistic, unworkable, impractical and not in accord with the facts of human nature if they had not been put in religious terms and therefore out of reach of any sound, sensible discussion, debate and resolution by scientific evidence.

Jesus is reported to have said (Matthew, 19, 9): "And I say to you: whoever divorces his wife, except for unchastity, and marries another, commits adultery." This is an unfortunate stance to take because it has led millions of people to feel guilty and a 'failure,' merely because they have been divorced. It is too narrow minded a view for any rational person to take. Divorce is surely a legitimate alternative in any rational consideration of married life. (Ard, 1977) The conventional view of monogamy, particularly the romantic, monogamous ideal as conceived in America, is surely destructive of many happy, realistic, healthy marriages.

>*"Almost the entire history of mankind demonstrates that man is not, biologically, a truly monogamous animal; that he tends to be more monogenous than monogamic, desiring one woman at a time rather than a single woman for a lifetime, and that even when he acts monogamously he craves strongly occasional adulterous affairs in addition to his regular marital sex. The female of the human species seems to be less strongly motivated toward plural sexuality than is the male; but she, too, when she can have varietistic outlets with social impunity, quite frequently takes advantage of them." (Albert Ellis, in Neubeck, 1969, p. 154)*

A rational consideration of the scientific evidence would seem to indicate that there are both healthy and disturbed reasons for having extramarital relations. (Albert Ellis, in Neubeck, 1969, pp. 153-161) Some of the healthy reasons, as outlined by Albert Ellis, are, sexual varietism, love enhancement, experiential drives, adventure seeking, sexual curiosity, social and cultural inducements and sexual deprivation. Some of the disturbed reasons are low frustration tolerance, hostility to one's spouse, self-depreciation, ego-bolstering, escapism and sexual disturbances. Dr. Albert Ellis has even published a book to help couples with this whole area. (Albert Ellis, The Civilized Couple's Guide to Extramarital Adventure, 1972) Once again, rather than assuming that this is something one has to do, a more rational stance would be to seriously consider the pros and cons, the various possible consequences, see what sort of an arrangement one can work out in a sane, reasonable and realistic fashion, and try to work out an agreement that is mutually arrived at, one that satisfied all the parties involved.

CHAPTER 7 REFERENCES

Ard, Ben N. Jr. "Monogamy: Is It Destructive of Marriage?
(Some Unconventional Thoughts on a Conventional Topic) The Marriage
and Family Counselors Quarterly, Vol. 7, pp. 1-8, 1972.

Ard, Ben N., Jr. "Sexuality as a Personal and Social Force," pp.
14-25, in Otto, Herbert (Editor) The New Sexuality. Palo Alto: Science &
Behavior Books, 1971.

Ard, Ben N., Jr. Treating Psychosexual Dysfunction. New York:
Jason Aronson, 1974.

Ard, Ben, Jr. "Love and Aggression: the Perils of Loving," pp.
286-295, in Ard, Ben N., Jr. & Ard, C. C. (Editors) Handbook of Marriage
Counseling. Palo Alto: Science & Behavior Books, 2nd edition, 1976.

Ard, Ben N., Jr. "Sex in Lasting Marriages: A Longitudinal
Study," The Journal of Sex Research, Vol. 13, No. 4, pp. 274-285,
November, 1977.

Baker, Robert &Elliston, Frederick (Editors) Philosophy & Sex.
Buffalo: Prometheus Books, 1975.

Comfort, Alex (Editor) The Joy of Sex. New York: Crown, 1972.

Ehrmann, Winston. "Marital and Nonmarital Sexual Behavior," pp.
585-622, in Christensen, Harold T. (Editor) Handbook of Marriage and the
Family. Chicago: Rand McNally, 1964.

Ellis, Albert. Sex Without Guilt. New York: Lyle Stuart, 1958.

Ellis, Albert. The Art and Science of Love. New York: Bantam
Books, 1966.

Ellis, Albert. "Healthy and Disturbed Reason for Having Extra-Marital
Relations," pp. 153-161, in Neubeck, Gerhard (Editor) Extramarital Relations.
Englewood Cliffs, N.J.: Prentice-Hall, 1969.

Englewood Cliffs, N.J.: Prentice-Hall, 1969.

Ellis, Albert. The Sensuous Person: Critique and Corrections.
Secaucus, N.J.: Lyle Stuart, 1972.

Ellis, Albert. The Civilized Couple's Guide to Extramarital
Adventure. New York: Wyden, 1972.

Gagnon, John H. Human Sexualities. Glenview, Illinois: Scott,
Foresman, 1977.

Harper, Robert A. & Stokes, Walter. 45 Levels to Sexual
Understanding and Enjoyment. Englewood Cliffs, N.J.: Prentice-Hall, 1971.

Hudson, John W. & Henze, Lura. "Campus Values in Mate Selection:
a Replication," pp. 73-79, in Wiseman, Jacqueline P. (Editor) People as
Partners. San Francisco: Canfield Press, 1971.

Lerner, Max. America as a Civilization. New York: Simon &
Schuster, 1957.

Masters, William H. & Johnson, Virginia E. Human Sexual
Response. Boston: Little, Brown, 1966.

Masters, William H. & Johnson, Virginia E. Human Sexual
Inadequacy. Boston: Little, Brown, 1970.

Pruette, Lorine. "Conditions Today," pp. 278-303, in Wile, Ira
S. (Editor) The Sex Life of the Unmarried Adult. New York: Vanguard
Press, 1934.

Taylor, Richard. Having Love Affairs. Buffalo: Prometheus
Books, 1982.

Young, Wayland. Eros Denied. New York: Grove Press, 1964.

"A rational study of divorce would seem to suggest that divorce might be thought of as an essential component of democracy. Just as there should be, in a democracy, no major abridgements of freedom of speech, assembly, and worship (including, as some moralists like to forget, freedom <u>not</u> to worship), just as there should be no attempt to prevent a person from <u>responsibly</u> taking and quitting a job rather than remaining forever in his first job, so, a critical judgment would seem to tell us, there should be no interference with a person's <u>responsibly</u> entering or leaving a marriage, rather than remaining forever in his first marriage."

Robert A. Harper

(in Ard & Ard, 1976, pp. 50-51)

CHAPTER 8
DIVORCE

Divorce has for so long been the ultimate wrong act in Western culture that even today when some liberalizations of the divorce laws have come about in the U.S., many people still have a great deal of trouble dealing with the ethical dilemmas involving divorce. The Judeo-Christian tradition has been against divorce for such a long time that many people today still feel guilty even considering divorce as a possible alternative.

How are sex and divorce related? Some people in this field would say that problems with sex lead to divorce in many, many cases. Louis Nizer, a noted lawyer, has reported that when he asks a client what he or she considers to be the basic reason for the marital crises,

> *"...I will get a whole catalogue of explanations from interference by in-laws to miserliness, and from drinking and gambling to temper tantrums. But when I probe long enough, the real reason emerges, and it is almost always the sexual relationship." (Louis Nizer, quoted in Slovenko, 1973, p. 350)*

The observation has been made that "In the two crucial human decisions to marry and to divorce knowledge and reason play the smallest part." (Slovenko, 1973, p. 355) If people were educated to be more rational in such matters, then these decisions could be leavened with some reasonable matters, then these decisions could be leavened with some reasonable considerations. More and more people are experiencing divorce these days. Some evidence is available that indicates that the number of divorces has doubled in the last ten years and tripled since 1950. If the divorce rate stabilized at the 1974 level it is estimated that over 40 per cent of the new marriages will ultimately end in divorce. (Ard, 1977)

It would seem, given these facts and trends, that we had better give up the "needle-in-the-haystack" theory of romantic love, i.e., the conventional view of lifelong monogamous marriage (or the concept that a human being can only truly love just one person in a lifetime). Divorce as a legitimate alternative provides a better, more rational option.

As the distinguished philosopher, Bertrand Russell, has put it, "...divorce should be possible without blame to either party and should not be regarded as in any way disgraceful...any marriage should be terminable by mutual consent..." (Bertrand Russell, in Seckel, 1987, pp. 223-224)

If one takes a more rational, realistic attitude toward love (and keeps open the possibility, at least, of loving more than one person in a lifetime), then one can face even the end of one love as no catastrophe. This would seem a saner, more sensible approach than the conventional view. (Ard, 1972)

Despite the fact that more and more people are getting divorces, a curious form of tolerance for divorce for other people seems to have developed. Even people who have gone through divorce themselves are sometimes only tolerant of divorce for others but not accepting of divorce for themselves as a legitimate, rational, indicated choice.

In a more rational scheme of things, divorce would be seen as a legitimate alternative, a reasonable choice, a decision which is rightly indicated under certain circumstances. In fact, divorce may be said to be the most rational decisions that could be made under certain circumstances. This would seem a more rational way of looking at this problem area, rather than arbitrarily defining divorce as a sin, or a failure, or a catastrophe, the end of the world, something for which one should feel guilty or ashamed. For some people, going through a divorce seems to "prove" to them that they are unlovable and therefore worthless as a human being. Psychotherapy is sometimes necessary to overcome these self-defeating and self-downing tendencies. The rational-emotive approach espoused by Dr. Albert Ellis and his colleagues (1962, 1971, 1973, 1975, 1977; Wolfe & Brand, 1977) is particularly apt and an effective, elegant way of resolving these sorts of problems.

In the rational-emotive approach to psychotherapy, one learns that it is rarely, if ever, the external, past situations that have occurred that cause the emotional consequences that are so self-defeating. In a useful, easy to remember scheme, the A-B-C of each situation can be conceptualized as follows: the external, past situation (called A) is practically never the real cause of the emotional consequences (called C), but there is an intermediate step (called B) in which the beliefs of the person come into play. The person's belief system, the way he or she defines the situation, the value assumptions, their philosophy of life, affects the way they see the situation and thus really causes the feelings or emotional consequences. The labeling process is really more important than the actual situation in that the labels hung on the situation really determine what the emotional reactions will be. In rational-emotive psychotherapy, the client is taught to conceptualize the situation in this fashion in order to learn to gain the serenity to accept the things he or she cannot change, the courage to change the things he or she can change, and the intelligence or wisdom to know the difference between the two. Another step, the D step, is for the person to dispute, question,challenge and change the irrational sentences he or she is telling himself or herself. This is a more elegant solution to the conventional views of divorce and helps a person change their philosophy of life.

We shall end this chapter with the words of the English philosopher, Bertrand Russell:

> *"The most usual ground for divorce ought to be one which is allowed in few countries, namely, mutual consent. The law of England, like that of New York state, lays it down that there shall be no divorce if both parties desire it. This is inherently absurd;" (Bertrand Russell, in Seckel, 1987, p. 308)*

CHAPTER 8 REFERENCES

Ard, Ben N., Jr. "Monogamy: Is It Destructive of Marriage? (Some Unconventional Thoughts on a Conventional Topic)" The Marriage and Family Counselors Quarterly, Vol. 7, pp. 1-8, 1972.

Ard, Ben N., Jr. "Beyond Divorce: What Then?" Rational Living, Vol. 12, No. 2, pp. 31-34, Fall, 1977.

Ellis, Albert. Reason and Emotion in Psychotherapy. New York: Lyle Stuart, 1962.

Ellis, Albert, et al. Growth Through Reason. Palo Alto: Science & Behavior Books, 1971.

Ellis, Albert. Humanistic Psychotherapy: the Rational-emotive Approach. New York: McGraw-Hill, 1973.

Harper, Robert A. "Moral Issues in Marital Counseling," pp. 48-57, in Ard, Ben N., Jr. & Ard, C. C. (Editors) Handbook of Marriage Counseling. Palo Alto: Science & Behavior Books, 2nd edition, 1976.

Seckel, A. (Editor) Bertrand Russell on Ethics, Sex and Marriage. Buffalo: Prometheus Books, 1987.

Slovenko, Ralph. Psychiatry and Law. Boston: Little, Brown, 1973.

Wolfe, Janet L. & Brand, Eileen (Editors) Twenty Years of Rational Therapy. New York: Institute for Rational Living, 1977.

"Unmarried adults are approaching sex as a fact rather than a theory. They are accepting their sexual organization frankly as an instrument for personal growth and emotional completion with stabilization, rather than hypocritically as a function designed by divine plan only for the procreation of pure beings whose excuse for living was that they might die in purity to attain happiness in a world to come. They appreciate that sex is the source of life, but believe that a sexless life is a mockery after biologic maturation, because it is contrary to nature."

Ira S. Wile (1934, p. 52)

CHAPTER 9
SEX AND THE UNMARRIED ADULT

For many, many years, the sex life of the unmarried adult in our culture was largely ignored because there was not supposed to be any. However, in one of the first books to deal with this heretofore ignored portion of the population, Ira Wile said,

> "The married people of the United States constitute the majority of those above the age of fifteen years; but approximately one-third of the people in the United States above the age of fifteen years are unmarried. The nature of the problem and the adjustments of so large a portion of the community cannot be ignored." (Wile, 1934, pp. xvi-xvii)

Who constitute the unmarried group in our culture?

> "Obviously it contains those who wish to be married and those who fear to be; those who should not, those who must not, those who cannot and those who may not; and those who can and may but reject marriage because of some specific factor, or are still in hopes of attaining matrimonial recognition." (Wile, 1934, p. 34)

XBy postulating sex within marriage as the only acceptable kind, conventional sex morality excluded normal sex from the lives of too many.

As the famous anthropologist Margaret Mead has said,

> *"Where both sexes are regarded as inherently,*
> *spontaneously, aggressively sexual from the time of*
> *puberty, society's insistence upon virginity at marriage or*
> *upon continence for the unmarried, results in coercion of*
> *almost every individual brought up in that society."*
> *(Margaret Mead, in Wile, 1934, p. 69)*

The conventional sex morality ignored reality by forbidding any sex outside of marriage. Continence for the unmarried was the only alternative offered. But as the famous physician Robert L. Dickinson has put it,

> *"The moralist insists that continence in the*
> *unmarried is wholly compatible with good health,*
> *unimpaired capacity for wonted work and reasonable*
> *serenity, and that there is no need for prescribing*
> *intercourse outside of marriage; it may be true, but the*
> *scientist is still asking for actual evidence and proof in*
> *place of mere opinion and he has not yet received it.*
> *There is considerable evidence that the male cannot arrest*
> *the activity of his glands or actually sublimate their*
> *function." (Robert L. Dickinson, in Wile, 1934, p. 202)*

Dr. Dickinson brought up in the quote just cited the concept of "sublimation," which has a long history in Western culture and was re-introduced by Freud. Sublimation was the only alternative offered to the unmarried, therefore we need to take a serious look at the concept.

Sublimation Forever?

Despite the fact that there is no scientific evidence to speak of to back up the psychoanalytical and conventional religious views of "sublimation," many people still believe that sexual desires can be satisfied in non-sexual ways. (Taylor, 1933) But sexual satisfaction cannot be gained by non-sexual means. Painting a picture of a nude, or doing some sculpture, or writing some music, will not bring the satisfaction of sexual intercourse. This is not to deny that there are satisfactions to be gained from various artistic and work endeavors, it is just that the satisfactions gained are not ones that satisfy human sexual desire, despite what the psychoanalysts and conventional religious moralists say.

We cannot simply tell the unmarried to sublimate their sexual desires. That is irrational and not realistic. As Lester A. Kirkendall has said, "The young can not be expected to sublimate their biology; they mature within a biological framework." (Kirkendall, in Grummon & Barclay, 1971, p. 288) Neither can anyone, of whatever age, be expected to gain sexual satisfaction from non-sexual means. If sex is a natural and normal part of life (as it would seem to be, rationally considered), then every individual has a right to some sex as a part of his or her life. The concept of sublimation is not backed up by scientific evidence and therefore deserved to be junked a long time ago but at least by now we had better be willing to throw out the concept of sublimation and recognize that everyone, married or unmarried, is entitled to sex in their life.

As the psychiatrist Donald J. Homes has noted, "To speak of the enjoyment of music, swimming, art, or conversation as 'forms of sexual pleasure' is misleading." (Holmes, 1972, p. 195) All these activities may be a part of one's work or pleasure activities but they are clearly not activities that can be substituted for sex. They are all sources of satisfaction, as is sex; they do not extinguish or substitute for each other. (Holmes, 1972, p. 195) In fact, in so far as we are rational and mentally healthy, we had better not get the various activities mixed up.

> "*Sublimation*, then, is not a matter of redirecting
> oral or phallic drives to higher purposes, but of learning
> how to do one thing at one time and another at another
> without getting them mixed up." (Holmes, 1972, p. 196)

If some people have a strong sex drive, they cannot realistically be simply told to "sublimate" it in nonsexual ways. "An extragenerous endowment of genital drive might contribute to mobilizing a person to do something, but it is doubtful that this something would diminish the need for genital discharge." (Holmes, 1972, p. 339)

It should be obvious from any serious consideration of the scientific evidence available that not everyone should be married or be a parent.

> "We should also recognize that marriage is not a
> feasible or desirable relationship for many persons because
> it calls for more than they can exhibit in the way of
> reciprocal interpersonal relationships, of concern for
> others, and of ability to develop and maintain a sustained,
> mutually fulfilling relationship with a person of the other
> sex. Likewise, parenthood is not desirable for many men
> and women who cannot develop the capacities for
> providing what a child should have to become a healthy
> personality." (Lawrence K. Frank, 1961, p. 168)

Many perfectly healthy people, who would make good parents, have chosen careers which practically preclude the time necessary to do a good job as a parent. So they may also opt for not getting married. But that hardly should mean that they must have no sex life and certainly does not call for any talk of sublimation or chastity.

> *"Chastity, in its old sense of sexual deprivation, can no longer, of course, be regarded as an essential value. Whether sexual development in the adult is experienced over time with one partner, or more than one, is a matter of circumstances and individual choice. There is more than one road to sexual fulfillment." (James Hemming, 1969, p. 246)*

In 1976, 42 percent of all new households in the United States were singles and only 13.5 percent were couples. (London, 1978, p. 40)

> *"The basic unit in today's society is the individual, who is able financially to live alone and find amiable companionship, sex, and other recreation, without having to provide anything more than that in return." (Perry London, 1978, p. 40)*

Sublimation should go the way of many other psychoanalytic concepts, into the garbage heap for lack of sufficient scientific evidence. The use of the concept of sublimation by many religious leaders to urge many young people to avoid sex has had many harmful consequences.

> *"The fact remains that young males are usually driven to some kind of orgasmic release and that, for their physical satisfaction as well as their growth and development as human beings, it is far better that they have their sex release with females than in most other*

outlets.

The idea that the human male can easily sublimate his sex desires into other more 'idealistic' channels is largely nonsense that is not supported by any factual evidence." (Albert Ellis, 1958, pp. 148-149)

Al Ellis also points out, recommending that, instead of having sex outlets, young males should take hot baths, run around the block, and so forth, simply will not work. (Albert Ellis, 1958, p. 149) Dr. William C. Taylor's famous monograph, A Critique of Sublimation in Males (1933) offers scientific evidence that we had better give up on the idea of sublimation.

According to another psychologist, Clarence Leuba, many women are likely to believe that sex can be dealt with satisfactorily before marriage through sublimation, having been taught this sort of idea by conventional sex moralists.

"The sexually experienced woman, however, usually develops strong cravings for the repetition of the erotic stimulations and satisfactions to which she has become accustomed. Such cravings may be more difficult to sublimate. Like the male's physiological tensions, they do not find adequate expression or gratification in such activities as painting and knitting! Sublimation never satisfies sexual cravings; at most, it may temporarily remove them from the center of attention." (Leuba, 1948, p. 75)

Various physical activities may tire a person out temporarily but that is hardly equivalent to satisfying their sexual urges.

> *"But sublimation is not a means of dissipating or satisfying the sexual desires themselves. Unless there is general exhaustion, the male's sexual desires may remain as strong as ever. The accumulated sperm and sexual fluids are not consumed by sublimation. The activities of sublimation distract the individual and dissipate restlessness, but they may leave the sex desires undiminished."* (Leuba, 1948, p. 76)

Finally, Leuba puts to rest that old canard about creative art work being sublimation or a substitute for sex:

> *"There is no evidence whatsoever that creative art work - or creative work of any sort for that matter - is particularly useful for purposes of sublimating sex. No activity, other than actual sexual functioning, will satisfy sexual desires..."* (Leuba, 1948, p. 76)

CHAPTER 9 REFERENCES

Dickinson, Robert L. "Medicine, " pp. 186-211, in Wile, Ira S. (Editor) The Sex Life of the Unmarried Adult. New York: Vanguard Press. 1934.

Ellis, Albert. Sex Without Guilt. New York: Lyle Stuart, 1958.

Frank. Lawrence K. The Conduct of Sex. New York: William Morrow: 961.

Hemming, James. Individual Morality. London: Panther Modern Society, 1970.

Kirkendall, Lester A. "Sex and Human Wholeness," pp. 278-290, in Grummon, Donald L. & Barclay, Andrew M. (Editors) Sexuality: A Search for Perspective. New York: Van Nostrand Reinhold, 1971.

Leuba, Clarence. Ethics in Sex Conduct. New York: Association Press, 1948.

London, Perry. "The Intimacy Gap," Psychology Today, Vol. 11, No. 12, pp. 40, 42-45, May, 1978.

Mead, Margaret. "Anthropology," pp. 53-74, in Wile, Ira S. (Editor) The Sex Life of the Unmarried Adult. New York: Vanguard Press, 1934.

Taylor, W. S. "A Critique of Sublimation in Males: A study of Forty Superior Single Men." Genetic Psychology Monographs. 13:1-115, 1933.

Wile, Ira S. (Editor) The Sex Life of the Unmarried Adult. New York: Vanguard Press, 1934.

"Once we realize that the primitive superego is merely a makeshift developmental mechanism, no more intended to be the permanent central support of our morality than is our embryonic notochord intended to be the central support of our bodily frame, we shall not take its dictates so seriously (have they not often been interpreted as the authentic Voice of God?), and shall regard its suppression by some more rational and less cruel mechanism as the central ethical problem confronting every human individual."

Julian Huxley (1947, p. 256)

CHAPTER 10
SEX AND GUILT

Perhaps many people, when asked what they think of when they feel guilty, would probably think of something to do with sex. In our culture particularly, sex and guilt have been tied together for so many years through the efforts of moralists. The results of tying sex and guilt together are many and devastating.

> "As psychoneurotics are uncommon among primitive people, part of the explanation of its prevalence among the civilized may rest upon the ideas of sin, guilt, shame and disgust, which arose from social forces crystallized in conscience." (Wile, 1934, pp. 37-38)

Traditionally in our culture, the conscience was assumed to be implanted in each person at birth and to be the voice of God speaking to the individual whenever he or she did anything wrong or sinful. Since conventional sex morality has had a long list of acts, deeds, and even thoughts and fantasies which were assumed to be evil, sinful, dirty and offenses against God and his commandments, the average person could hardly do (or even think) much about sex without feeling guilty.

Freud came along and postulated that the conscience was not inborn at birth but rather developed as a "superego" early in life. This was perhaps a step forward over the previous ideas about conscience but all was not well, even then. Freud divided the human being into id (unconscious), out of which developed the ego (conscious, executive part of the personality) and superego (or largely unconscious conscience). Freud and the psychoanalysts who followed him treated matters of conscience or superego somewhat differently than did moralists.

> *"There is a difference, however, between the analyst and the moralist. In battling to release the productive forces in the individual the analyst is on the side of the ego, not the super-ego, nor merely the id. In this weary world of reality (it is not a nursery, Freud repeatedly assures us) he strives to help the individual find realistic ways of living that are not energy-destroying, pleasure-robbing, instinct denying. And in this attempt he may find himself pitted against a phoney super-ego, impossible standards, infantile prohibitions." (Cole, 1953, p. 852)*

Of course, there are psychoanalysts, psychiatrists and psychologists who do continue to side with the conventional moralists, for example, Karl Menninger, William Glasser, and O. Hobart Mowrer, to mention only a few. (Ard, Living Without Guilt and/or Blame, 1983, Chapter 6) Karl Menninger, a psychiatrist, has sought to re-introduce the concept of sin in his recent book, Whatever Became of Sin? (1973) Mowrer has also collected together and edited a series of papers on Morality and Mental Health (1967) as well as having suggested elsewhere (1964) that science gives no support for morality and virtue. Mowrer has suggested that counselors should become actively concerned with "unredeemed sin" and thereby "help" their clients to admit their "real guilt" and to seek "atonement." (Mowrer, 1964, p. 750)

It should be obvious that any rational consideration of these matters would force one to other conclusions. The return to a "moralistic" counseling as advocated by Mowrer, Menninger, Glasser, et al, would not best meet the needs of counselors or their clients in our pluralistic society. In fact, it would be a return to the Dark Ages. (Ard, Counseling and Psychotherapy, 1975, p. 410)

Fortunately there are other psychologists and psychiatrists who take a more rational view. As psychiatrist Donald Holmes has put it,

> *"As a child-rearing measure, guilt-conditioning is an expedient, over-generalized substitute for more rational teaching by demonstration, precept, and explanation. In time we may even be able to discard the superego idea, with its implication of a biologically based and definitive ethos." (Holmes, 1972, p. 220)*

Radical as the idea of giving up the superego as the basis for making ethical decisions may be, it is the hope of the future. (Ard, Living Without Guilt and/or Blame, 1983) As Holmes says,

> *"That we must behave well in various ways is accepted, but that guilt feeling, confession, expiation, and penance are good and necessary to this end is an unfounded proposition." (Holmes, 1972, p. 220)*

The psychoanalysts introduced the concept of "identification" to explain how the superego developed in the growing child. But once again, we need to take a more critical look at this psychoanalytic assumption:

> *"The identification concept of moral*

> *growth...precludes the possibility of a child's moral growth*
> *- through independent observation, learning, and thinking*
> *- beyond the highest attainment of his elders."* *(Holmes,*
> *1972, p. 222)*

There are alternative ways, more rational ways, to conceive of how children can learn to make ethical decisions. (Ard, 1983, Chapter 9)

> *"Ideally, however, we try to go beyond guilt and*
> *shame to more rational motives for self-determined*
> *behavior. An excess of guilt or shame detracts from the*
> *pleasure of living and even defeats its own aims."*
> *(Holmes, 1972, p. 225)*

The psychiatrist Donald Holmes offers these final words of wisdom:

> *"As we live in a community of people with competing*
> *interests, we must have some internalized blueprints to*
> *direct our behavior; but conscience and superego are only*
> *two of the many possible. They are in the tradition of*
> *unquestioning reality to arbitrary authority."* *(Holmes,*
> *1972,p. 225)*

Perhaps one of the clearest and most outspoken statements on this matter of guilt comes from the psychologist Albert Ellis:

> *"The fact is, therefore, that literally millions of*
> *Americans, including untold numbers of college students,*
> *are still exceptionally guilty about sex in general and*
> *premarital affairs in particular. Is this good? I say, as*

definitely and as unequivocally as I can, that it is not.
Guilt, when accurately defined, is virtually always
irrational, self-defeating, and evil. In relation to sex
behavior, it is particularly idiotic. I have spent a good
part of the last quarter of a century crusading against
it;..." (Albert Ellis, in Grummon & Barclay, 1971, p. 227)

Merely lessening the severity of the superego or conscience, as some of our Freudian colleagues suggest, will not accomplish the necessary task. We will need to seek out a more thoroughgoing, a more fundamental, a more elegant solution. The superego or conscience is a sturdy weed and merely cutting it back, so to speak, or pruning it a bit here and there, will not get at roots. People need to get at their unquestioned philosophical assumptions which underlie, and ultimately cause, their injustice collecting and their guilt.

If we want to get at the crux of the matter regarding guilt and the related concept of justice, no better source can be found than the ideas of Walter Kaufmann, the philosopher, who has spelled out his analysis of these two concepts in his book <u>Without Guilt and Justice</u> (1973).

Kaufmann has made a searching philosophical analysis of the concepts of guilt and justice and teaches us a way to live in a very irrational world, a world that is not "fair" (and may never be), where one cannot realistically expect, or certainly not demand, absolute or perfect justice. Kaufmann says that when we are willing to give up this demand for absolute or perfect justice, then the tyranny of guilt comes to an end. For without this demand for perfect justice, there need be no guilt. Seeking perfection leads to guilt when we inevitably fall short; giving up on perfectionism leads to no need to feel guilty.

Kaufmann has clearly pointed out to us that guilt feelings are a contagious disease that harms those who harbor them and also endangers those who live close to them. Guilt feelings are a form of resentment. The person who harbors them is therefore a menace. Only reason can decide what is irrational. The conscience or superego is not a rational source for value decisions. Kaufmann has clearly shown that guilt feelings are irrational. To liberate ones-self, one had better break the chains of guilt.

How is the best way to go about breaking the chains of guilt? Psychotherapy may ultimately be the best way, at least for those reared in such a way as to engender a heavy load of guilt. Psychoanalysis has tried to cut down on the severity of the superego but has not completely faced the full implications of the problem. (Ard, Living Without Guilt and/or Blame: Conscience, Superego and Psychotherapy, 1983)

The Superego

Psychoanalytic thought conceives of the superego (and others conceive of the conscience) as a natural, normal part of human beings. The mature ego, according to Freud, remains subject to the superego's domination. (Freud, 1927, p. 69) Even though psychoanalytic therapy attempts to make the ego more independent of the superego (Freud, 1933, pp. 111-112), there is evidently no attempt to eliminate the superego entirely.

However, the complete elimination of the superego in the psychologically healthy adult would seem to be a better, ultimate aim. Freud, in stating the object of therapeutic efforts, said "Where id was, there shall ego be." (Freud, 1933, pp. 111-112) Fenichel capably adds what definitely needs to be added, that this dictum should be supplemented. We had better also say that "where superego was (i.e., the automatic autonomy of unreasonable guilt feelings, the principle of talion, revenge, and automatisms), "there shall ego be" (i.e., a reasonable handling of reality). Fenichel wisely comments that such an additional "shall" runs up against socially determined barriers. (Fenichel, 1945, p. 589) This is a masterpiece of understatement! But we had better simply work harder to overcome such barriers. The present book, hopefully, is a step in that direction. (Cf., also, Ard, Living Without Guilt and/or Blame: Conscience, Superego and Psychotherapy, 1983)

Throughout the ages there have been rebellious individuals who have held that the spontaneous human impulses are better than people have usually been willing to believe (misled by their own institutions and traditions), and that moral control, whether exercised by an external authority or by internal conscience, has tended to suppress and distort much of this natural goodness. (Flugel, 1945, p. 245) Maslow (1971) might be a good recent example of this sort of thing.

"Self-alienation may be summed up in a word - guilt - a word with which both religion and psychiatry are closely involved. Guilt intrudes one way or another. Hence the cure for much self-alienation is the purging of guilt." (James Hemming, 1969, p. 172)

Karen Horney has recognized the inadequacy of the Freudian position with regard to the superego. She has offered another and better way of looking at these phenomena. For Freud the superego is a normal phenomena representing conscience and morality; it is neurotic only if particularly cruel and sadistic. For Horney the equivalent "shoulds" and taboos of whatever kind and degree are altogether a neurotic, counterfeiting morality and conscience. (Horney, 1950, p. 374) As she has so succinctly put it:

> *"Freud can aim merely at reducing the severity of*
> *the superego while I aim at the individual's being able to*
> *dispense with his inner dictates altogether and to assume*
> *the direction of his life in accordance with his true*
> *wishes and beliefs. This latter possibility does not exist*
> *in Freud's thinking." (Horney, 1950, p. 375)*

The orthodox psychoanalysts and most other psychotherapists have in the main thought only in terms of the reduction of the severity of the superego (Post, 1972); the need for the complete elimination of the superego is a stand which they evidently cannot bring themselves to even consider (if they have ever even considered such a thought), it would seem. Hence they unwittingly advocate the retention of some infantile traits, with no clear awareness that trading with the devil, so to speak (that is, the superego), no matter how carefully safeguarded, merely keeps him alive and likely at any occasion to erupt full force into action. There can be no successful compromise with the superego, a fact not sufficiently appreciated by many psychoanalysts, social workers, psychologists, counselors or laypeople.

One of the factors perhaps contributing to this apparent inability of many professional people to come to eliminating the superego probably lies in their dislike of allowing "value judgments" to enter into their professional work. But some value judgments are essential on the part of professional workers (if they are working to help their clients achieve full psychological maturity, or mental health). This is, of course, anathema to many if not most such professional workers. Sigmund Freud and Carl Rogers are strange bedfellows (being the leaders of the opposing "directive" and "non-directive" schools of thought) but they both seem to agree in trying to keep value judgments out of therapy (ultimately).

Now in one sense this is perfectly legitimate and even necessary: the therapist had better be free from any tendency to condemn the client or "moralize" at the client. But Erich Fromm has only pointed out what would seem to be equally obvious, and that is, that "the analyst's convictions about what is good for man must play some part in his goal of therapy." (Quoted in Thompson, 1950, p. 210) And, as Julian Huxley has said, we need

> *"the achievement of sufficient psychological understanding and control to enable the bulk of mankind, or at least the leaders in every field, to take the resolution of their intrinsic moral conflict a stage further than before, to a point at which punishment, whether of self or others, is no longer constantly demanded to appease the tension of inner guilt." (Huxley & Huxley, 1947, p. 248)*

A standard of right and wrong, built up childishly in childish years, and vested in the superego, is not enough for a better civilization. (Grace Stuart, Conscience and Reason, 1951, p. 121) We can do better and develop alternatives to the superego in matters of ethical decisions. As Flugel has put it:

> *"Man is indeed fundamentally a moral animal. But we have also learnt that much of this morality is crude and primitive, ill adapted to reality, and often at variance both with his intellect and with his higher conscious aspirations...his social institutions and traditions exhibit an*

> *inertia that makes them often out of harmony with the requirements of a rapidly changing civilization, so also his moral constitution is in many respects ill suited to his present cultural needs. Progress in each case demands an abandonment of the old and maladaptive features."*
> *(Flugel, Man, Morals and Society, 1945, pp. 240-241)*

And speaking directly to the question at hand regarding the superego, Flugel concludes:

> *"If we seek, therefore, to achieve a morality that is free as regards feeling and behavior as well as free from metaphysical constraints, it is not sufficient to abandon what we may consider outworn superstitions and beliefs as regards the external aspects of the Universe. We have also to free ourselves from the archaic aspects of our own internal superego." (Flugel, 1945, p. 188)*

There is little doubt that the direction of evolution is towards a restriction of the importance of the superego, and an increase in the power and freedom of reason. (Waddington, The Scientific Attitude, 1948, p. 165) We do not need to merely sit back and await these developments, we had better work as hard as we can in these directions.

> *"We all have to think as hard as we are able, accepting the challenge that any problem we are intelligent enough to envisage as a problem we are capable of thinking about. The hard struggle of life is to get the thinking straight and to act from the straight thinking." (James Hemming, 1969, p. 256)*

A society where no superego is built automatically into the child will not be one necessarily wherein the people will "run wild" (or run amok), nor one in which there will be no inner ethical conflict. But this ethical conflict (rather than a moral conflict) will, ideally, reach a somewhat higher level of resolution: a level at which the emotionally neutral power of the intellect, supported by experience and the scientific attitude, is exerted to release some of the knotted emotional tensions of the superego. (Julian Huxley, 1947, p. 244) This is an essential stage in the passage of the individual to ethical and psychological maturity. It involves the substitution of unconscious (superego) motivation by rational, conscious (ego), ethical motivation. As Waddington has put it, in a scientific society, "The superego would be the interloper." (Waddington, The Scientific Attitude, 1948, p. 166)

Short of extensive psychoanalysis, however, which we have seen might not do the job of complete extirpation of the superego, there are methods of psychotherapy that can do the elegant job thoroughly. The psychologist Albert Ellis, with his rational-emotive therapy, has offered effective help in this regard.

> "In summary, if you can think about the things that precede or accompany your guilt, discover your own philosophic assumptions with which you make them bother you, and forcefully and consistently challenge and dispute these assumptions, you will stop feeling guilty about anything you do - particularly sex acts." (Ellis, 1976, p. 79)

By applying the rational-emotive approach to one's thinking, feeling and acting (behaving), one can learn not to feel guilty, particularly about committing sex acts which conventional sex morality arbitrarily defines as sinful, evil or wrong. No one need continue to feel guilty or to blame themselves or others for any sex acts. If one has committed certain sex acts which one does not want to repeat, then the question is always, "How can I so act in the future that will be the ethical way I would prefer to act?"

According to the rational-emotive approach,

> *"Guilt keeps you from doing what you enjoy, and can make you a salve to others. Downing yourself, which is a major part of guilt, is never necessary." (Ellis & Becker, A Guide to Personal Happiness, 1982, p. 85)*

It never helps to blame oneself, even for acts which are wrong in one's own estimation, all things considered. One can hold oneself <u>accountable</u> FOR THOSE THINGS OVER WHICH ONE HAS SOME CONTROL, but no one can rationally be blamed for events for which they have little or no control. Responsibility or <u>accountability</u> are a necessary part of a rational person's ethical philosophy of life; <u>blaming</u> is <u>not</u> a necessary part of a sane, rational philosophy of life.

Guilt is also not a necessary part of the way a rational person works out an ethical decision. A psychologically mature person can live sane, sensible, reasonable life <u>without a superego</u>, WITHOUT FEELING GUILTY, and certainly without <u>blaming</u> ANYONE FOR ANYTHING, particularly oneself. Developing a rational sex ethics will go a long way toward helping individuals lead such lives.

CHAPTER 10 REFERENCES

Ard, Ben N., Jr. "Nothing's Uglier Than Sin," pp. 409-415, in Ard, Ben N., Jr. (Editor) Counseling and Psychotherapy. Palo Alto: Science & Behavior Books, revised edition, 1975.

Ard, Ben N., Jr. "The Conscience or Superego in Marriage Counseling," pp. 610-67, in Ard, Ben J., Jr. & Ard, C. C. (Editors) Handbook of Marriage Counseling. Palo Alto: Science & Behavior Books, 2nd edition, 1976.

Ard, Ben N., Jr. Living Without Guilt and/or Blame: Conscience, Superego and Psychotherapy. Smithtown, N.Y.: Exposition Press, 1983.

Cole, Lawrence E. Human Behavior. Yonkers-on-Hudson: World Book, 1958.

Ellis, Albert. Sex Without Guilt. New York: Lyle Stuart, 1958.

Ellis, Albert. "Sex Without Guilt," pp. 226-244, in Grummon, Donald L. & Barclay, Andrew M. (Editors) Sexuality: A Search for Perspective. New York: Van Nostrand Reinhold, 1971.

Ellis, Albert. Sex and the Liberated Man. Secaucus, N.J.: Lyle Stuart, 1976.

Ellis, Albert & Becker, Irving. A Guide to Personal Happiness. North Hollywood: Wilshire Book Co., 1982.

Finichel, Otto. The Psychoanalytic Theory of Neurosis. New York: Norton, 1945.

Flugel, J. C. Man, Morals and Society. New York: International Universities Press, 1945.

Freud, Sigmund. The Ego and the Id. London: Hogarth Press, 1927.

Freud, Sigmund. New Introductory Lecturers on Psycho-analysis.

160

Freud, Sigmund. <u>New Introductory Lecturers on Psycho-analysis</u>. New York: Norton, 1933.

Hemming James. <u>Individual Morality</u>. London: Panther Modern Society, 1970.

Holmes, Donald J. <u>Psychotherapy</u>. Boston: Little, Brown, 1972.

Horney, Karen. <u>Neurosis and Human Growth</u>. New York: Norton, 1950.

Huxley, T. H. & Huxley, Julian. <u>Touchstone for Ethics</u>. New York: Harper, 1947.

Kaufmann, Walter. <u>Without Guilt and Justice</u>. New York: Wyden, 1973.

Menninger, Karl. <u>Whatever Became of Sin?</u> New York: Hawthorn, 1973.

Mowrer, O. Hobart. "Science, sex and values," <u>Personnel and Guidance Journal</u>, April, 1964, 746-753.

Mowrer, O.Hobart (Editor) <u>Morality and Mental Health</u>. Chicago: Rand McNally, 1967.

Post, Seymour C. (Editor) <u>Moral Values and the Superego Concept</u>. New York: International universities Press, 1972.

Stuart, Grace. <u>Conscience and Reason</u>. New York: Macmillan, 1951.

Thompson, Clara. <u>Psychoanalysis: Evolution and Development</u>. New York: Hermitage, 1950.

Waddington, C. H. <u>The Scientific Attitude</u>. New York: Penguin Books, 2nd edition, 1948.

Wile, Ira. S. (Editor) <u>The Sex Life of the Unmarried Adult</u>.

New York: Vanguard Press, 1934.

"I would tend to recommend, therefore, that we stop speaking about sex deviations at all, that we drop the nasty, pejorative connotations that almost invariably go with the use of such terms, and that instead we merely try to distinguish between sexual (and nonsexual) behavior that occurs in an emotionally disturbed manner."

Albert Ellis (1976, pp. 285-286)

CHAPTER 11
PROBLEMATIC SEXUAL BEHAVIOR

Not too many years ago, the material to be covered in this chapter would have been said to concern "sexual perversions," a term which has fallen out of favor in recent years in the field. Even the term "sexual deviance," which has somewhat replaced the older term "perversion," has some connotations which some people think are unfortunate, to say the least. Paraphilias is another term used for these sorts of behaviors. The question reduces to what is considered "normal" or "abnormal." Rather than introduce too many terms which are heavily laden with moral assumptions, the term "problematic sexual behavior" will be used herein. (Ard, 1974, pp. 157-170)

Although we need not make any moralistic judgments about people who exhibit problematic sexual behavior, this does not mean that no value judgments can be legitimately made in this area at all. It is still helpful to inquire as to what are the consequences for a person of a given pattern of sexual behavior, and whether the behavior contributes to or detracts from the person's happiness in the long run.

The various patterns of sexual behavior that are usually considered in this context include, for example, bestiality, homosexuality, S & M (sadism and masochism), transvestitism (cross-dressing), transsexualism, necrophilia and pedophilia, fetishism, etc. In the on-going sexual revolution, several of these areas have become quite "political" in recent years, as we shall see.

The whole area of homosexuality in particular has been receiving considerable attention of late, what with the development of a gay liberation or homophile movement (Sacarides, 1975, pp. 81-112) and several philosophical discussions have appeared in the professional literature. (Atkinson, 1965, pp. 132-141; Baker & Elliston, 1975, pp. 247-302; Albee, et al, 1983; Aries & Bejin, 1986)

Homosexuality

Recently the American Psychiatric Association was pressured into changing their classification of homosexuality. In the diagnostic manual published by the APA homosexuality was formerly listed as a psychiatric disorder under "sexual deviations." Henceforth, after the 1973 vote, homosexuality was defined as a "sexual orientation disturbance." As Margolis (in Baker & Elliston, 1975, p. 290) has stated, "Clearly, the attempt of the APA to accommodate prevailing changes in personal convictions threatens to undermine the entire foundation of the manual."

Various authorities in the field hold differing views on the nature of homosexuality. Bieber, for example, holds heterosexual functioning to be injured by homosexuality; he holds that in all homosexuals there has been a disturbance of normal heterosexual development, although he does not claim that such a disturbance is always behaviorally manifested, or even felt as subjective distress. He seems to regard the so-called "satisfied" homosexual as even more disturbed than the homosexual upset with his own condition. (Margolis, in Baker & Elliston, 1975, p. 292)

In a definitive book on the subject, Homosexuality: Its Causes and Cure (1965), Dr. Albert Ellis has said:

> "...in spite of the early and later contention by any

outstanding authorities that homosexuality is fundamentally
inborn and that it is therefore almost impossible to
change the basic sexual drive of a confirmed or exclusive
homosexual, the opposing view of the psychoanalytic
schools, that homophilism is largely an early-acquired
sexual anomaly, and that despite the stubborn resistance
to change of most homosexuals their sexual proclivities
sometimes can be definitely changed in the direction of
heterosexual interests and activities, has fairly well
conquered the field of psychiatric thinking and is
subscribed to by the great majority of psychotherapists."
(Ellis, 1965, pp. 21-22)

Another psychologist, Lorine Pruette, has given a very apt description of what homosexual relations do for the individual's involved:

"Homosexual relations cut the individual off from the
main current of social life and subject him to all the
undesirable development which appear in any group which
feels itself discriminated against and maltreated. Where a
definite cult develops, with delusions of superiority to the
vulgar, "normal" mob, proselyting tendencies are also
likely to appear, which in part explains society's
repugnance to such groups." (Lorine Pruette, in Wile,
134, p. 295)

Lorine Pruette also points out an ethical position which is certainly more rational than some of the conventional "moral" positions frequently encountered in some religious leaders:

> *"If we do not accept the theory of biological*
> *inevitability, it would seem that society's best defense*
> *against such groups lies not in hounding or oppressing the*
> *individual homosexual, but in seeking to develop more*
> *satisfactory sexual relations between men and women and*
> *more wholesome family life from which the children will*
> *gain their own norms of behavior." (Lorine Pruette, in*
> *Wile, 1934, p. 295)*

Harold Greenwald, in his book <u>Direct Decision Therapy</u> (1974) has claimed that homosexuals have made decisions regarding their homosexual pattern of sexual activity. Some homophiles do not like the implications of Greenwald's view, i.e., that they are <u>responsible</u> for the sexual pattern they have decided upon and that they could choose to decide differently. Assuming that their sex pattern is innate, that they were born that way and cannot possibly change, relieves them of any responsibility for their style of life. But if the facts are different, then this is a cop-out, an attempt to avoid taking charge of their lives.

Ethical decisions regarding homosexuality (and other problematic sexual behavior) are complex and difficult because they may include prudential considerations, many philosophical assumptions and aesthetic factors as well as certain styles of life. As Joseph Margolis has put it:

> *"Or, values regarding personal development and*
> *personal relationships that are neither clearly moral nor*
> *prudential - possibly, in some serious sense, aesthetic*
> *values regarding the quality of life - may be claimed to*
> *be affected: homosexuality and other so-called*

perversions may be said to threaten the 'richness' or
'fullness' or 'style' or 'quality' of life by diverting our
tastes into narrower, more restricted or less than fully
'human' options." (Margolis, in Baker & Elliston, 1975, p.
296)

Presenting some of the possible negative conclusions about homosexuality will probably cause the gay activists or homophiles to assume that rational sex ethics are therefore "against" homosexuals. As Socarides (1975, p. 87) has pointed out in discussing recent development regarding homosexuality, "...militant homosexual groups continued to attack any psychiatrist or psychoanalyst who dared to present his finding as to the psychopathology of homosexuality before national or local meetings of psychiatrists or in public forums." Despite the efforts of the homophile groups, homosexuality cannot rationally be touted as simply an acceptable variation of the norm, an alternative life-style to heterosexuality. Homosexuals may choose to continue the life-style they prefer, and as long as they do not force themselves on others, or seduce minors, or defeat their own ends or goals, they may be said to have, in some sense, a "right" to continue their chosen life-style with other consenting adults. But rational sex ethics would preclude seducing minors, or forcing their unwanted attentions on anyone, on the part of homosexuals (just as the same considerations would apply to heterosexuals, under a more rational scheme of ethics). Condemning or blaming homosexuals for their sexual behavior is rarely, if ever, helpful. Offering psychological and philosophical help to those homosexuals who would like to examine the long-term consequences of their style of life would seem to be a lot more rational than the usual stance of conventional sex morality.

A very high percentage of confirmed homosexuals have what Dr. Paul Meehl calls cognitive slippage, as Dr. Albert Ellis has pointed out (Sex and the Liberated Man, 1976, p. 295), in spite of their high intelligence, and find great difficulty making some of the finer discriminations required for adequate social relations.

> "They have exceptionally low opinions of themselves, think negatively a good deal of the time, and constantly damn themselves and others. They frequently feel depressed, have low energies, act in a disorganized fashion, feel unspontaneous and anhedonic, feel woefully dependent upon others, constantly upset themselves over little things, and have relatively little fun in life except when under the influence of alcohol, drugs, or other stimulants. For the most part, they act in a highly obsessive-compulsive manner, particularly in regard to cruising for sex partners and for love partners, and have great difficulty finding the latter on any kind of a steady basis, because they mainly obsess themselves with receiving love and proving how worthwhile that makes them, rather than with loving." (Albert Ellis, Sex and the Liberated Man, 1976, pp. 295-296)

Transvestitism

Cross-dressing, or dressing up in the clothes of the other sex occurs as a pattern in some men's lives on rare occasions, sometimes only at home (i.e., never in public), and often makes for no change in their sex life. In other words, they may lead a sex life that is no different than "normal" heterosexual men except for their cross-dressing. Such men certainly may be said to have the "right" to dress in this fashion in so far as it harms no one else. Some cross-dressers, however, want to cross-dress and appear in public and be accepted as a woman. Compulsiveness, however, sometimes enters in and frequently causes many transvestites to have problems resulting from their cross-dressing. Where cross-dressing involves homosexuality then the previous comments about homophiles would still apply. The rational objections to transvestitism relate to the obsessive-compulsive quality that frequently is involved.

Fetishism

When some men become obsessively and compulsively fascinated more in a fetish (e.g., women's shoes or panties) in a way that precludes having satisfying sexual intercourse, they are seen by some professionals as having a sexual problem. But in these days of ultra-liberals in sexual matters, some people assume that all people with a fetish have just as much right to their style of life as anybody, since they harm nobody. Once again, a rational sex ethics would agree that anyone has a "right" in some sense to use whatever means to sexual satisfaction he wants, as long as it is not harmful to anyone. Most fetishes fall into this category since they tend to be inanimate objects. But further questions remain: is a pattern of sexual behavior rational which in effect is one wherein a man can only achieve sexual satisfaction with some fetish? What are the long-term consequences of this pattern of sex life? The fetishist would seem to have a rather limited view of sex; once again a person has a "right" to collect women's shoes or panties and use them in masturbation, but it may not be the wisest pattern of sexual behavior possible.

Transsexualism

Probably one of the most serious patterns of sexual behavior and thinking which tests the ultra-liberal to the utmost is the transsexual who wants surgical intervention to change his or her sex organs to those of the other sex. Rational sex ethics, again, would hold the view that a person, given the proper circumstances as spelled out at such places as Johns Hopkins and Stanford medical schools (where these operations have been performed), has a "right" to seek out any surgery they want, provided they have rationally considered all the probable consequences of the various alternatives. One of the major difficulties here is that transsexual surgery is not reversible. (Meyer, 1976) If a "mistake" is made, there is nothing that can be done about it then. And as Harold Greenwald has stated,

> *"Most of the transsexuals I know about did not have any chromosomal difference, or any other discoverable physical difference. Their 'need' to change seems to have been entirely psychological." (Greenwald, 1974, pp. 265-266)*

Transsexual surgery will probably continue to pose serious ethical dilemmas for all concerned because, once the decision to operate has been made and the operation completed, the person cannot then decide to reverse the procedure (if they decide then that they have made a mistake in having the operation).

Paraphilias

Having sex with animals, infants, small children, corpses and various inanimate objects are all possibilities and do occur among some people. The radical position on these matters, or the ultra-liberal stance, is that anyone should be allowed to do whatever they want to do sexually. However, careful analysis of all aspects of the matter may call for some other conclusions, if we want to be consistently rational. As Thomas Nagel has stated,

> "...various familiar deviations constitute truncated or incomplete versions of the complete configuration and may therefore be regarded as perversions of the central impulse." (Thomas Nagel, in Baker & Elliston, 1975, p. 256)

If we see the development of normal sexual patterns as something that occurs in stages, then we can agree with Thomas Nagel that "intercourse with animals, infants, and inanimate objects seem to be stuck at some primitive version of the first stage." (Nagel, in Baker & Elliston, 1975, p. 256)

> "The concept of perversion can hardly fail to be evaluative in some sense, for it appears to involve the notion of an ideal or at least adequate sexuality that the perversions in some way fail to achieve. So, if the concept is viable, the judgment that a person or practice or desire is perverted will constitute a sexual evaluation, implying that better sex, or a better specimen of sex, is possible." (Nagel, in Baker & Elliston, 1975, p. 258)

However, we want to be crystal clear that such evaluations are <u>not</u> moralistic judgments (not questions of sin or breaking some supposedly divine laws or commandments) but rather much like other sorts of judgments that we make on a very naturalistic basis. As Nagel has said, "We make judgments about people's beauty or health or intelligence that are evaluative without being moral." (Nagel, in Baker & Elliston, 1975, p. 259)

>*"Finally, even if perverted sex is to that extent not so good as it might be, bad sex is generally better than none at all. This should not be controversial: it seems to hold for other important matters, like food, music, literature, and society. In the end, one must choose from among the available alternatives, whether their availability depends on the environment or on one's own constitution. And the alternatives have to be fairly grim before it becomes rational to opt for nothing." (Nagel, in Baker & Elliston, 1975, p. 259)*

This particular argument may be difficult for some to accept but when one considers that there are a lot of men, for example, who for a variety of reasons (such as physical handicaps, ugliness, illnesses, etc.) would have considerable difficulty obtaining sex in the normal or usual fashion, and thus may turn to various unusual forms of sexual behavior for some satisfaction, then it would seem rational to allow for such patterns of sexual behavior, provided, of course, that no harm is done to anyone in the process. This would preclude, therefore, sex between old men and children (pedophilia) because the two are not equal and the child can not give what could be termed informed consent (the kind that can occur between two consenting, equal adults).

Some of the problematic sexual behaviors, or paraphilias, can occur between men and prostitutes, for example, and where this behavior is mutually agreed to and harms no one, then a rational sex ethics would not rule out such behavior. This does not mean, however, that such behaviors might not be eliminated if the men wanted to eliminate them in favor of something better. The various sex therapists that are available these days can provide just such professional assistance when it is desired or indicated. (Ard, 1974; Kaplan, 1974; Ellis, 1976; Masters & Johnson, 1970; Masters, Johnson & Kolodny, 1977)

CHAPTER 11 REFERENCES

Albee, George; Gordon, Sol; Leitenberg, Harold (Editors)
Promoting Sexual Responsibility and Preventing Sexual Problems.
Hanover: University Press of New England, 1983.

Ard, Ben N., Jr. Treating Psychosexual Dysfunction. New York:
Jason Aronson, 1974.

Aries, Philippe & Benjin, Andre (Editors) Western Sexuality.
New York: Basil Blackwell, 1986.

Atkinson, Ronald. Sexual Morality. New York: Harcourt, Brace &
World, 1965.

Baker, Robert & Elliston, Frederick (Editors) Philosophy & Sex.
Buffalo: Prometheus Books, 1975.

Ellis, Albert. "Another Look at Sexual Abnormality," pp. 151-158,
in Ellis Albert. Sex Without Guilt. New York: Lyle Stuart, 1958.

Ellis Albert. Homosexuality: Its Causes and Cure. New York:
Lyle Stuart, 1965.

Ellis, Albert. Sex and the Liberated Man. Secaucus, N.J.: Lyle
Stuart, 1976.

Greenwald, Harold. Direct Decision Therapy. San Diego: Edits, 1974.

Kaplan, Helen Singer. The New Sex Therapy. New York:
Quadrangle, 1974.

Margolis, Joseph. "The Question of Homosexuality," pp. 288-302,
in Baker, Robert & Elliston, Frederick (Editors) Philosophy & Sex.
Buffalo: Prometheus Books, 1975.

Masters, William H. & Johnson, Virginia E. Human Sexual
Inadequacy. Boston: Little, Brown, 1970.

Masters, William H.; Johnson, Virginia E.; Kolodny, Robert C.

Masters, William H.; Johnson, Virginia E.; Kolodny, Robert C.
Editors) <u>Ethical Issues in Sex Therapy and Research</u>. Boston: Little,
Brown, 1977.

Meyer, Jon K. (Editor) <u>Clinical Management of Sexual Disorders</u>.
Baltimore: Williams & Wilkins, 1976.

Nagel, Thomas. "Sexual Perversion," pp. 247-260, in Baker,
Robert & Elliston, Frederick (Editors) <u>Philosophy & Sex</u>. Buffalo:
Prometheus Books, 1975.

Pruette, Lorine. "Conditions Today," pp. 278-303, in Wile, Ira
S. <u>The Sex life of the Unmarried Adult</u>. New York: Vanguard, 1934.

Socarides, Charles W. <u>Beyond Sexual Freedom</u>. New York:
Quandrangle Books, 1975.

"Again, the ethics of sex relations is filled with so many taboos that it is extremely difficult to overcome habitual prejudices even when psychological considerations have made it clear that we must change some of our traditional valuations if we want happier and healthier men and women. In all such cases, the cognitive result has to be supported by a readjustment of our volitional attitudes." (Hans Reichenbach, <u>The Rise of Scientific Philosophy</u>, 1951, p. 299)

CHAPTER 12
SCIENCE AND ETHICS

We have seen in the foregoing chapters that sexual matters can be (and have been for too long a period of time) approached from a moralistic, supernatural, religious point of view. However, as this book has tried to demonstrate, sexual matters can also be approached from an ethical point of view, one that has been termed rational or scientific or naturalistic. In fact, this whole book is an attempt to integrate sex and ethics in a rational, democratic, scientific manner.

The scientific point of view has been suggested in this book to be the preferred way to decide ethical questions, rather than the mystical, supernatural, religious and moralistic ways which have traditionally decided questions of sexual morality. In a conference on reason and morality in London in 1984 (Overing, 1985), attended by social anthropologists and philosophers, it was agreed by these philosophers that the cognitive skills developed by Western scientists are superior to all others in the history of the world, and such skills had better be the yardstick by which we measure and judge all others. (Overing, 1985, pp. 1-2) Hollis and Newton-Smith, for example, go so far as to lable mistaken beliefs, those that the methods of Western science would not validate, as 'irrational beliefs.'" (Overing, 1985, p. 2)

Netwon-Smith, in his book The Rationality of Science (1981), has clearly pointed out that it is very much in our interest to act on true beliefs. As pointed out that it is very much in our interest to act on true beliefs. As he says, "If I generally act on false beliefs the chances of realizing my goals will be adversely affected." (Newton-Smith, 1981, p. 242)

> "To achieve the goal of having true beliefs it is in
> my interest to take reasonable steps to acquire evidence
> and to assess the evidence shrewdly. In condemning a
> belief as not rational we are claiming that the believer
> did not take reasonable steps to acquire the relevant
> evidence and/or that he did not asses the evidence
> satisfactorily." (Newton-Smith, 1981, p. 242)

It is hoped that even though different readers as individuals, might differ with some of the specific conclusions reached on various issues in the previous pages, the main line of the argument has been convincing, namely that one can become more rational in handling the ethical matters involving sex. This chapter will take a concluding look at the overall arguments about the relationship between science and ethics.

Do We Need Sermons or Science?

As more scientific evidence is discovered, some of the conclusions reached in earlier chapters may need to be revised, as is customary in scientific circles where there are no "absolutes" and the commitment to the scientific attitude means a willingness to change your attitudes when presented with scientific evidence. But scientific, not supernatural, considerations will be the guide for all future ethics which are truly rational. As Maslow has stated:

> "To spell out only one implication here, these
> propositions affirm the existence of the highest values

within human nature itself, to be discovered there. This
is in sharp contradiction to the older and more customary
beliefs that the highest values can come only from a
supernatural God, or from some other source outside
human nature itself." (Maslow, Toward a Psychology of
Being, 1968, p. 170)

So one of the conclusions or theses of this book is that we had better stop using religious or supernatural considerations for making so-called <u>moral</u> decisions about sex and start using scientific considerations to make <u>ethical</u> decisions in a more rational manner.

If someone were to exercise his or her choice and refuse to act rationally but followed instead conflicting dictates of "faith" or "instinct," then the question that must be decided is whether or not the person means to act in his or her best interest.

"If he does, but his actions, prompted by nonrational
considerations, conflict with the dictates of rationality,
then his actions are <u>self-defeating</u>. He aims to do
something, but goes about it the wrong way." (John
Kekes, A Justification of Rationality, 1976, p. 169)
[Emphasis added.]

"But given that human beings are what they are,
such a policy cannot be pursued for long. It leads either
to death or to inconsistency." (John Kekes, A
Justification of Rationality, 1976, p. 169)

The philosopher John Kekes has devoted a whole book to his justification of rationality, and we cannot go into the detail that he does, but we can state one of his basic conclusions:

> *"But given human nature and the environment,*
> *rationality is a matter of necessity. For human nature and*
> *the environment jointly make it inevitable that human*
> *beings have problems which they must solve, and*
> *rationality is the method for solving them. The standards*
> *of rationality are simply the formulation of the most*
> *promising rules of problem-solving." (John Kekes, A*
> *Justification of Rationality, 1976, p. 169)*

Erich Fromm has shown in his book Man For Himself (1974) that the sources of norms for ethical conduct may be found in man's nature itself; that ethical norms should be based upon man's inherent qualities, and that violation of these norms results in mental and emotional disintegration. (Fromm, 1974, p. 7)

A psychiatrist, Donald Holmes, has said,

> *"There is no use denying any longer that*
> *psychiatrists also teach ethics, not as a rigid catechism to*
> *be memorized and held like a magical holy stone, but as*
> *an attitude toward self and other people that will increase*
> *the pleasure of all." (Holmes, Psychotherapy, 1972, p.*
> *1029)*

For too long now too many people have attempted to keep science (which entails facts) and values or ethics (or actions) entirely separated. But as the philosopher Ronald Atkinson has pointed out:

> *"Our actions bring about changes in the physical and*
> *social world in which we live, and consequently facts*

about that world and the effects of our actions in it are
relevant to the assessment of our actions." (Atkinson,
1965, p. 182)

Many people are disturbed by the current ongoing sexual renaissance or
sexual revolution and some people obviously believe that we can reinstate or
enforce more rigorously our conventional sex morality and that will solve the
problem at hand. However, as Lawrence K. Frank wisely observed in his book
The Conduct of Sex (1961),

"A few, however, are aware of the need for
exploring other possible ways of establishing and
maintaining social order and regulating human behavior,
not only for orderly group living, but for the sake of the
individuals who, as personalities, need to be free from the
coercion of their own organic functions and impulses, and
free from their persistent feelings of guilt, anxiety and
resentment, able to, live at peace with themselves and so
at peace with others, as one human personality relating to
other personalities. Not many, however, are prepared to
explore these possibilities which call for a critical
examination of what kinds of personalities we shall seek
for what kind of social order."

"The issue we face, therefore, involves a number of
questions concerned with our conceptions of human nature
and of social order, and the place and the meaning of sex
in human living and in the development of personalities.
Since these questions so often challenge our long-

established traditional concepts and assumptions, they usually provoke strong, if not violent, emotional reactions." (Lawrence K. Frank, 1961, pp. 142-143)

"The scientist must on occasion question many of the premises on which current conventional morality is based. A student of society is a sorry failure, if, after years of scientific study, he has the same conceptions about a problem area as the man in the street. (Ard, in Farber & Wilson, 1967, p. 95) It is the scientist's task to be analytical and critical about believes, and if he fails in this he fails in everything. As Erich Fromm has pointed out in <u>Man For Himself</u> (1947), where he discussed the contradiction between the conventional morality of our society and the ethics necessary for the psychologically mature person, "It is the obligation of the student of the science of man not to seek for 'harmonious' solutions, glossing over this contradiction, but to see it sharply." (Fromm, 1947, p. 244)

Many people these days think that the scientific approach is "neutral," or, put another way, that science has nothing to say about good or evil, right or wrong, morality or ethics. These people imply that what is good and what is evil cannot be judged by the standards of science. Science, they say, tells us only what is true and what is false; they insist that true and false are quite different standards from good and evil. But as J. Bronowski has pointed out, this separation of the true and the false from good and evil is destructive of social ethics. (J. Bronowski, <u>A Sense of the Future</u>, 1977, p.

197) For it removes ethics from the tests by which we judge the things that happen around us every day, and makes it something remove from our practical lives.

> *"This is most dangerous now, when the setting of our lives is being changed by discoveries in medicine, in mental health, in psychology, and in social science in ways which most affect the relations between human beings. Our habits, particularly our habits of thought, are shifting profoundly. In such a time it is a disaster to think that the difference between knowledge and ignorance is somehow more trivial than the difference between good and evil." (J. Bronowski, 1977, p. 201)*

Just what, specifically, do we mean by the scientific approach? As Lester Kirkendall has spelled it out,

> *"One important consequence of the scientific approach is to teach us to question what is not clear. The concern for gathering facts, to determine cause and effect, to know both immediate and long-range consequences, to think rationally on all issues, and to understand the principles which operate in any particular situation these are part and parcel of the scientific method." (Kirkendall, in Wiseman, 1976, p. 393)*

The present book on rational sex ethics, like the book Toward a Psychology of Being (1968) written by A. H. Maslow, is unmistakably a normative social psychology. And, like Maslow's book, has a different point of view regarding science than is frequently encountered in the field.

> *"That is, it accepts the search for values as one of the essential and feasible task of a science of society. It is thus in direct contradiction to that orthodoxy which excludes values from the jurisdiction of science, claiming in effect that values cannot be discovered or uncovered by can only be stated arbitrarily, by fiat, by non-scientists." (Maslow, 1968, p. 220)*

There has arisen of late an anti-intellectualism, an anti-science point of view which turns out, ultimately, to be anti-reason. This recent movement is not the first that such anti-reason or anti-science tends have come about in Western culture.

> *"So there has repeatedly arisen an expression of hatred for all scientific, rational, forms of thought. Now it takes the form of praise for the poetical, metaphorical, more primitive form of feeling (rather than conceptualizing) one's way into life... Or it may take the form of a strong advocacy of a return to a more religious outlook on life." (Cole, 1953, p. 643)*

We need to be forewarned against any such return to a religious outlook:

> *"But there are also world-weary religions, decadent philosophies, religions that express (and at the same time reinfect the sick soul with) poisonous doubt, guilt, fear, deepening the sense of frustration and despair out of which they arise. There are philosophies that are cynical, 'know-nothing,' confessions of man's impotence, of the meaninglessness of life, of the futility of striving. There*

are philosophies and religions of escape, of other-
worldliness, of denial. CAVEAT EMPTOR!" (Cole, 1953, p.
845)

Lester Kirkendall has suggested that we need to reconceptualize sex in
terms of human wholeness. He has also expressed a very open frankness
about continued discussions of morality.

> *"Once we are able to think this way, basically we*
> *will be thinking positively of human fulfillment, of joyous*
> *responsibility in relations that create a sense of worth*
> *and self-respect in all who are parties to them. And we*
> *can cease our discussions of morality -- I, for one, am*
> *sick of them. The more I think of human growth and*
> *fulfillment and what is involved in the realization of*
> *potentials, the more discussions of traditional morality*
> *seem to me comparable to discussions about sorcery and*
> *witchcraft. Away with them! On with learning what is*
> *involved in loving and caring for people." (Kirkendall, in*
> *Grummon & Barclay, 1971, p. 289)*

Kirkendall is not the only leader in the field who has come out against
morality. The distinguished scientist Raymond B. Cattell has even written a
book on A New Morality from Science: Beyondism (1972). In his book
Cattell has described the possibilities of developing a system of ethics from
science. As he says,

> *"...our larger and more radical task here is to show*
> *how ethics may be developed for society out of science,*
> *not to bring the existing revealed ethics of society into*

> *science. Its aim is to develop a basis for moral values as a special <u>branch</u> <u>of science</u>, rooted in the objectivity of science itself." (Cuttell, 1972, p. 38) [Emphasis in original.]*

Some people still like to think that we need to accept the intuitive insights from art, literature and religion, particularly where sex is concerned. They believe that science cannot give us any help with values. But as Cattell has said,

> *"...the only dependable path toward clarifying that which art and religion seek to understand is the path of scientific method." (Cattell, 1972, p. 31)*

Whether we should follow the dictates of religion or the findings of science, whether we need more sermons or more science, Cattell has concluded that

> *"...modern science should be capable, in principle, of guiding progress in moral values as positively as other fields of progress, eliminating the need to depend on the <u>a priori</u> assertions of revealed religion." (Cattell, 1972, p. 52)*

What shall be the basis of a rational sex ethics? Cattell says

> *"Although the difficulties are very great, we have to voyage in search of a new scientific, i.e., <u>combined</u> <u>rational</u> <u>and</u> <u>empirical</u> basis for finding ethical values which is uniform with our scientific procedure in understanding nature generally." (Cattell, 1972, p. 64) [Emphasis in original.]*

Thus rational sex ethics offers us a way out of the morass of morality.

The conventional sex morality based on a religious stand merely means a set of moral principles that some church arbitrarily insists in God's word, imposes on all individuals and defines as good and correct. (Albert Ellis, in Grummon & Barclay, 1971, p. 235) Secular humanism, on the other hand, as Albert Ellis states,

> "...posits a set of ethical principles that the humanists believe, on logical-empirical grounds, is probably correct, that they think is good for most of the people much of the time, and that they are quite willing to modify if subsequent experience proves that they lead to undesirable (meaning self-defeating or humanity-defeating) results." (Albert Ellis, in Grummon & Barclay, 1971, pp. 235-236)

Religionists, on the other hand, as Albert Ellis has pointed out, tend to believe that sex is sacred and holy, that it was invented by God for the purpose of propagating His creation, that man has a spirit or soul that is entirely divorced from his body, and that he is nobler and wiser when he becomes preoccupied with this spirit and experiences physical pleasures only in a highly subjugated way.

> "But their believing these hypotheses hardly gives such theories any plausibility or validity. As a scientist and an atheist, I prefer to believe that such hypotheses are clearly unprovable and are most probably hogwash. As a highly experienced psychotherapist, moreover, I have considerable reason to suspect that a dogmatic belief in any kind of supernaturalism and a preoccupation with the

realm of spirit rather than full acceptance of the joys of the flesh are more than a little nutty, and that, in fact, intense and orthodox religiosity is little more than another name for what we ordinarily call severe emotional disturbance or mental illness." (Albert Ellis, in Grummon & Barclay, 1971, p. 238)

Therefore, in the light of the above findings, it does not seem reasonable to suppose that a good way to resolve our current ethical dilemmas with regard to sex is to "return to religion" and the old ways of handling such matters.

"Although some believe that the historically developed moral code can be re-established and made effective by more stringent laws and severe penalties and threats of punishment, this does not seem probable or desirable in view of what our traditional sex morality has brought in the way of hypocrisy, evasion, and sex offenses, to say nothing of the immense toll of personality problems and human defeats." (Lawrence K. Frank, The Conduct of Sex, 1961, p. 175)

More hope for the future will be possible if we turn to reason, the scientific approach, rather than religion. We do not need more sermons, but rather more science. As Freud said,

"Our best hope for the future is that the intellect the scientific spirit, reason should in time establish a dictatorship over the human mind. The very nature of reason is a guarantee that it would not fail to concede to

human emotions and to all that is determined by them,
the position to which they are entitled.... Whatever, like
the ban laid upon thought by religion, opposes such a
development is a danger for the future of mankind."
(Freud, 1933, pp. 234-235)

Science, or the scientific approach, cannot fully account for everything
we might like at a given moment. There is always an area of uncertainty
remaining, it seems. But when confronted with remaining uncertainty,
ambiguity, or unknowns, we have essentially two choices, as the psychiatrist
Roderic Gorney, in discussing the future of The Human Agenda *(1972), has*
pointed out.

"We can either assume that the phenomena imply an
unbridgeable disjuncture from the rest of the universe and
demand a supernatural interpretation, or we can compose
ourselves and work persistently until science can deliver
new understanding. The most persuasive reason for making
the latter choice is of course that past success of science
in unraveling other tangles. But a close second is
provided by the failure of revelation to do so. Of course,
since health is on the same side, it is also compatible
with the mature personality to side with patience rather
than petulance." (Roderic Gorney, 1972, p. 566)

The rational approach to sex ethics proposed in the present book can
help organize life experiences meaningfully, just as concepts of nutrition and
disease transmission have helped lay people take scientifically valid rather
than magical or superstitious precautions against disease. High school

students need to learn scientifically valid means of birth control (rather than using such invalid methods as Saran wrap or Coke douches, for example) and high school youth can be taught how to make rational ethical decisions, as evidenced by the work being done by Dr. Margaret Arcus and her colleagues at the University of British Columbia in Vancouver. (Coombs, 1971, 1975)

Making Rational Judgments

Can we teach people to make rational value judgments? Two organizations have made extensive efforts in this direction: the Institute for Rational-Emotive Therapy in New York City (and several branches in North America and Europe) and the Association for Value Education and Research (A.V.E.R.) in the Faculty of Education at the University of British Columbia, Vancouver, British Columbia, Canada.

A.V.E.R has concentrated on school-based values education and has completed a sizeable experiment in junior secondary schools. A.V.E.R. has also been involved in multidisciplinary research on values and has developed materials and procedures whereby people, especially young people, can develop competence in making rational value judgments, decisions and choices.

A.V.E.R. states that it is the case that young people lack rational means of dealing with the bewildering range of value choices that confronts them in modern society. Obviously, the outcome to be sought is not that students will have been indoctrinated in any particular value positions, but that they will have acted according to certain standards of reasoning in arriving at judgments and decisions. As A.V.E.R. states:

"This implies, of course, that there are standards of
reasoning for determining which values are worth holding

and which are not. Many will disagree with this assertion. Values, they argue, are 'merely matters of opinion' or 'nothing more than expressions of feelings'. Of course, if they are correct, value changes can be neither defended nor criticized, and if value conflicts occur, they can be settled only by persuasive appeals to emotions or by force. We believe that, at least for some value areas, these people are mistaken; that in some value areas it is possible to give adequate reasons for holding to some values while disavowing other values. To put this another way, we believe that it is possible to be rational about some of one's values." (Introduction to the aims and activities of A.V.E.R., no date.)

The error of the anti-scientific values people, the error they make, is to assume that all values are nothing more than tastes. We had better distinguish between indoctrinating people and educating them. There is a difference between the two approaches, and it is a significant difference.

The whole task of clarifying the nature of value judgments is to describe exactly how we reason from facts to value conclusions. Jerrold Coombs, of the University of British Columbia, has analyzed this problem clearly in several publications. (Coombs, 1971, 1975) His work is drawn on heavily in what follows immediately.

Value Analysis

Making a value judgment commits the evaluator to a value judgment because his or her judgment logically implies a principle. Anyone making a value judgment commits himself or herself to: (1) a value principle, and (2) a set of facts about the value object which shows that the principle applies to the value object. The facts and the value principle comprise the premises of a deductive argument having the value judgment as its conclusion.

We arrive at an evaluation on the basis of relevant facts. To be relevant to a value decision, facts have to meet two conditions: (1) they must be facts about the value object, and (2) they must be facts to which the evaluator ascribes some value rating.

What are the standards of rational value judgment? Jerrold Coombs has spelled out four:

Standards of Rational Value Judgment

It is now possible to specify in general terms the conditions which a value judgment must meet to quality as rational or defensible.

"1. The purported facts supporting the judgment must be true or well confirmed.

2. The facts must be genuinely relevant, i.e., they must actually have valence for the person making the judgment.

3. Other things being equal, the greater the range of relevant facts taken into account in making the judgment, the more adequate the judgment is likely to be.

4. The value principle implied by the judgment must be acceptable to the person making the judgment."
(Coombs, 1971, p. 18)

The fourth standard of rationality derives from the fact that one cannot accept a value judgment and reject the value principle implied by it without involving himself or herself in a logical contradiction. A rational way of determining the acceptability of a value principle is by trying to find reasons, i.e., relevant facts and more general value principles, which justify it.

Teaching Rational Living

At the Institute for Rational-Emotive Therapy in New York City, Dr. Albert Ellis and various of his colleagues have been teaching school children in a private school run by the Institute how to be more rational in their lives. The Institute also has open meetings at which the general public is introduced to rational thinking and how to conduct their everyday lives on a more rational basis. Specifically referring to the subject matter of the present book, or trying to help people lead more sane sex lives, Dr. Albert Ellis has stated

"Sexual sanity (like nonsexual sanity), then, largely consists of noncompulsiveness, of personal experimentation, of open mindedness, of sticking to pathways that do not entail too many practical disadvantages, and perhaps above all, of accepting yourself and utterly refusing to down yourself even if you do the wrong thing and indubitably behave self-defeatingly."
(Albert Ellis, 1976, p. 300)

The crux of the matter as far as rationally deciding whether or not a given sex act is truly wrong or not is succinctly put by Dr. Albert Ellis thusly:

"We may call a sex act truly wrong by exactly the same rule we use for a nonsexual act -- if it needlessly

harms or takes unfair advantage of another human being.
If it only proves self-harming, then it is wrong in the
sense of its indicating self-defeatism or neurosis." (Albert
Ellis, 1976, p. 78)

The rational approach that Dr. Albert Ellis and his colleagues have developed has grown widely in the over twenty years since its inception. (Ellis & Grieger, 1977, 1986; Wolfe & Brand, 1977) Now there are Institutes of Rational Living or Institutes of Rational-Emotive Therapy in various cities in this country and also in Europe.

These institutes not only provide psychotherapy for both individuals and groups through their clinical staffs, they also provide lectures and workshops and education for the public. There are several books written specifically for the laypublic which serve to introduce this rational approach to life. (Ellis & Harper, 1975; Ellis, 1975; Ellis, 1977; Ellis & Becker, 1982) All in all, it would seem that one can learn to be more rational about sex, that one can develop a rational sex ethic. It is hoped that the present book has introduced that possibility to the reader along with a wealth of resources into which one may delve if one is really interested in developing one's own rational sex ethics.

CHAPTER 12 REFERENCES

Ard, Ben N., Jr. "Gray Hair for the Teenage-Father," pp. 95-104,
in Farber, Seymour & Wilson, Roger H. L. (Editors) Teenage Marriage
& Divorce. Berkeley: Diablo Press, 1967.

Atkinson, Ronald. Sexual Morality. New York: Harcourt, Brace &
World, 1965.

Bronowski, Jacob. A Sense of the Future: Essays in Natural
Philosophy. Cambridge: The MIT Press, 1977.

Cattell, Raymond B. A New Morality from Science: Beyondism.
New York: Pergamon Press, 1972.

Cole, Lawrence E. Human Behavior. Yonkers-on-Hudson: World
Book 1953.

Coombs, Jerrold R. "Objectives of Value Analysis," pp. 1-28, in
Metcalf, Lawrence F. (Editor) Values Education: Rationale, Strategies,
and Procedures. (National Council for the Social Studies 41st Yearbook,
1971)

Coombs, Jerrold R. "Concerning the Nature of Moral Competence,"
pp. 7-20, in Society for the Study of Education. The Teaching of
Values in Canadian Education, Volume 2, 1975.

Ellis, Albert. "Sex Without Guilt," pp. 226-244, in
Grummon, Donald L. & Barclay, Andrew M. (Editors) Sexuality: A
search for Perspective. New York: Van Nostrand Reinhold, 1971.

Ellis, Albert. How to Live with a 'Neurotic.' New York: Corwn,
revised edition, 1975.

Ellis, Albert. Sex and the Liberated Man. Secaucus, N. J.:
Lyle Stuart, 1976.

Ellis, Albert. How to Live With and Without Anger. New

Ellis, Albert. How to Live With and Without Anger. New
  York: Reader's Digest Press, 1977.

Ellis, Albert & Harper, Robert A. A New Guide to Rational
  Living. Englewood Cliffs, N. J.: Prentice-Hall, 1975.

Ellis, Albert; Grieger, Russell, et al. Handbook of Rational-Emotive
Therapy. New York: Springer, Volume I, 1977, Volume II, 1986.

Ellis, Albert & Becker, I. A Guide to Personal Happiness. North
  Hollywood: Wilshire Books, 1982.

Frank, Lawrence K. The Conduct of Sex. New York: Morrow, 1961.

Freud, Sigmund. New Introductory Lectures on Psychoanalysis.
  New York; Norton, 1933.

Fromm, Erich. Man For Himself. New York: Rinehart, 1947.

Gorney, Roderic. The Human Agenda. New York: Simon & Schuster,
  1972.

Holmes, Donald J. Psychotherapy. Boston: Little, Brown, 1972.

Kirkendall, Lester A. "Sex and Human Wholeness," pp. 278-290, in
  Grummon, Donald L. & Barclay, Andrew M. (Editors) Sexuality: A
  Search for Perspective. New York: Van Nostrand Reinhold, 1971.

Kirkendall, Lester A. "Sex and Social Policy," pp. 385-406,
  in Wiseman, Jacqueline (Editor) The Social Psychology for Sex. New
  York: Harper & Row, 1976.

Kekes, John. A Justification of Rationality. Albany: State
  University of New York Press, 1976.

Maslow, A. H. Toward a Psychology of Being. Princeton, N. J.
  Van Nostrand, second edition, 1968.

Overing, Joanna (Editor) <u>Reason and Morality</u>. London: Tavistock, 1985.

Newton-Smith, W. H. <u>The Rationality of Science</u>. London: Routledge & Kegan Paul, 1981.

Reichenbach, Hans. <u>The Rise of Scientific Philosophy</u>. Berkeley: University of California Press, 1951.

"Read, every day, something no one else is reading. Think, every day, something no one else is thinking...It is bad for the mind to be always a part of unanimity."
Christopher Morely

BIBLIOGRAPHY

Albee, George; Gordon, Sol; Leitenberg, Harold (Editors) Promoting Sexual Responsibility and Preventing Sexual Problems. Hanover, Vermont: University Press of New England, 1983.

Alexander, Richard D. The Biology of Moral Systems. Hawthorne, N. Y.; Aldine de Gruyter, 1987.

American College Health Association. Making Sex Safer. (Pamphlet) Rockville, Maryland: American College Health Association, 1987.

Ard, Ben. "Do As I Do, Be As I Am: The Bruising Conflict," pp. 78-88, in Farber, Seymour M. & Wilson, Roger H. L. (Editors) Sex Education & The Teenager. Berkeley: Diablo Press, 1968a.

Ard, Ben. "Gray Hair for the Teen-age Father," pp. 95-104, in Farber, Seymour M. & Wilson, Robert H. L. (Editors) Teenage Marriage & Divorce. Berkeley: Diablo Press, 1967b.

Ard, Ben N., Jr. "Sexuality as a Personal and Social Force," pp.14-25, in Otto, Herbert (Editor) The New Sexuality. Palo Alto: Science & Behavior Books, 1971.

Ard, Ben N., Jr. "Monogram: Is It Destructive of Marriage? (Some Unconventional Thoughts on a Conventional Topic)," The Marriage and Family Counselors Quarterly, Vol. 7, pp. 1-8, 1972.

Ard, Ben N., Jr. "Premarital Sexual Experience: A Longitudinal Study," Journal of Sex Research, Vol. 10, No. 1, pp. 32-39, February, 1974.

Ard, Ben N., Jr. Treating Psychosexual Dysfunction. New York: Jason Aronson, 1974.

Ard, Ben N., Jr. "Are All Middle-class Values Bad?", pp. 351-356, in Ard, Ben N., Jr. (Editor) Counseling and Psychotherapy: Classics on Theories and Issues. Palo Alto: Science & Behavior Books, revised edition, 1975.

Ard, Ben N., Jr. "Nothing's Uglier Than Sin," pp. 409-415, in Ard, Ben N., Jr. (Editor) Counseling and Psychotherapy: Classics on Theories and Issues. Palo Alto: Science & Behavior Books, revised edition, 1975.

Ard, Ben N., Jr. "The Conscience or Superego in Marriage Counseling," pp. 61-67, in Ard, Ben N., Jr. & Ard, C. C. (Editors) Handbook of Marriage Counseling. Palo Alto: Science & Behavior Books, 2nd edition, 1976.

Ard, Ben N., Jr. "Love and Aggression: the Perils of Loving," pp. 286-295, in Ard, Ben N., Jr. & Ard, C. C. (Editors) Handbook of Marriage Counseling. Palo Alto: Science & Behavior Books, 2nd edition, 1976.

Ard, Ben N., Jr. "Different Sexual Patterns in Marriage," pp. 389-395, in Ard, Ben N., Jr. & Ard, C. C. (Editors) Handbook of Marriage Counseling. Palo Alto: Science & Behavior Books, 2nd edition, 1976.

Ard, Ben J., Jr. Living Without Guilt and/or Blame: Conscience, Superego and Psychotherapy. Smithtown: N. Y.: Exposition Press, 1983.

Aries, Phillippe & Bejin, Andre (Editors) Western Sexuality. New York: Basil Blackwell, 1986.

Atkinson, Ronald. Sexual Morality. New york: Harcourt, Brace & World, 1965.

Bainton, Roland H. What Christianity Says About Sex, Love and Marriage. New York: Association Press, 1957.

Bainton, Roland H. "Christianity And Sex: An Historical Survey," pp. 17-96, in Doniger, Simon (Editor) Sex and Religion Today. New York: Association Press, 1953.

Baker, Robert & Elliston, Frederick (Editors) Philosophy & Sex. Buffalo: Prometheus Books, 1975.

Barnes, Harry Elmer. The Twilight of Christianity. New York: Vanguard Press, 1929.

Barnes, Harry Elmer. Society in Transition. New York: Prentice-Hall, 1939.

Bassett, Marion. A New Sex Ethics and Marriage Structure. New York: Philosophical Library, 1961.

202

Baumrin, Bernard H. "Sexual Immorality Delineated," pp. 116-128, in Baker, Robert & Elliston, Frederick (Editors) Philosophy & Sex. Buffalo: Prometheus Books, 1975.

Bayles, Michael D. "Marriage, Love, and Prostitution," pp. 190-266, in Baker, Robert & Elliston, Frederick (Editors) Philosophy & Sex. Buffalo: Prometheus Books, 1975.

Beigel, Hugo G. Encyclopedia of Sex Education. New York: William Penn, 1952.

Blanshard, Paul. American Freedom and Catholic Power. Boston: Beacon Press, 1949.

Briffault, Robert. "Sex in Religion," pp. 31-52, in Calverton, V. F. & Schmalhausen, S. D. (Editors) Sex in Civilization. Garden City, N. Y.: Garden City, 1929.

Bronowski, Jacob. A Sense of the Future: Essays in Natural Philosophy. Cambridge: The MIT Press, 1977.

Cattell, Raymond B. A New Morality from Science: Beyondism. New York: Pergamon Press, 1972.

Cavan, Ruth S. The American Family. New York: Crowell, 1953.

Cohen, Carl. "Sex, Birth Control, and Human Life," pp. 150-165, in Baker, Robert & Elliston, Frederick (Editors) Philosophy & Sex. Buffalo: Prometheus Books, 1975.

Cole, Lawrence E. Human Behavior. Yonkers-on-Hudson: World, 1953.

Cole, William Graham. Sex in Christianity and Psychoanalysis. New York: Oxford University Press, 1955.

Comfort, Alex. Sexual Behavior in Society. New York: Viking, 1950.

Coombs, Jerrold R. "Objectives of Value Analysis," pp. 1-28, in Metcalf, Lawrence E. (Editor) Values Education: Rationale, Strategies, and Procedures. (Natural Council for the Social Studies 41st Yearbook, 1971).

Coombs, Jerrold R. "Concerning the Nature of Moral Competence," pp7-20, in Society for the Study of Education. The Teaching of Values in Canadian Education, Volume 2, 1975.

Dearborn, Lester, "Masturbation," pp.356-367, in Fishbein, Morris & Burgess, E. W. (Editors) Successful Marriage. Garden City, N. Y.: Doubleday, 1948.

Dickinson, Robert L. "Medicine," pp. 186-211, in While, Ira S. (Editor) The Sex Life of the Unmarried Adult. New York: Vanguard Press, 1934.

Ditzion, Sidney (Editor) <u>Marriage, Morals and Sex in America</u>. New York: Bookman, 1953.

Doniger, Simon (Editor) <u>Sex and Religion Today</u>. New York: Association Press, 1953.

Ehrmann, Winston. "Marital and Nonmarital Sexual Behavior." pp.535-622, in Christensen, Harold T. (Editor) <u>Handbook of Marriage and the Family</u>. Chicago: Rand, McNally, 1964.

Ellis, Albert. <u>The American Sexual Tragedy</u>. New York: Twayne, 1954.

Ellis, Albert. <u>Sex Without Guilt</u>. New York: Lyle Stuart, 1958.

Ellis, Albert. <u>Reason and Emotion in Psychotherapy</u>. New York: Lyle Stuart, 1962.

Ellis, Albert. <u>Homosexuality: Its Causes and Cure</u>. New York: Lyle Stuart, 1965.

Ellis, Albert. "Healthy and Disturbed Reasons for Having Extra-marital Relations," pp. 153-161, in Neubeck, Gerhard (Editor) <u>Extramarital Relations</u>. Englewood Cliffs, N. J.: Prentice-Hall, 1969.

Ellis, Albert. "Sex Without Guilt," pp. 226-244, in Grummon, Donald L. & Barclay, Andrew M. (Editors) <u>Sexuality: A Search for Perspective</u>. New York:

Van Nostrand Reinhold, 1971.

Ellis, Albert. The Sensuous Person: Critique and Corrections. Secaucus, N. J.: Lyle Stuart, 1972.

Ellis, Albert. Humanistic Psychotherapy: the Rational-Emotive Approach. New York: McGraw-Hill, 1973.

Ellis, Albert. How to Live with a 'Neurotic'". New York: Crown, revised edition, 1975.

Ellis, Albert. Sex and the Liberated Man. Secaucus, N. J.: Lyle Stuart, 1976.

Ellis, Albert. How to Live With and Without Anger. New York: Reader's Digest Press, 1977.

Ellis, Albert & Grieger, Russel, et al. Handbook of Rational-Emotive Therapy. New York: Springer, 1977.

Ellis, Albert & Harper, Robert A. A New Guide to Rational Living. Englewood Cliffs, N. J.: Prentice-Hall, 1975.

Ellis, Albert & Becker, Irving. A Guide to Personal Happiness. North Hollywood: Wilshire Book Co., 1982.

Ellis, Albert; Greiger, Russell, et al. Handbook of Rational-Emotive Therapy.

206

New York: Springer, Volume I, 1977, Volume II, 1986.

Fenichel, Otto. The Psychoanalytic Theory of Neurosis. New York: Norton, 1945.

Fletcher, Joseph. "A Moral Philosophy of Sex." in Doniger, Simon (Editor) Sex and Religion Today. New York: Association Press, 1953.

Flugel, J. C. Man, Morals and Society. New York: Wiley, 1943.

Ford, C. S. & Beach, F. A. Patterns of Sexual Behavior. New York: Harper, 1951.

Frank, Lawrence K. Nature and Human Nature. New brunswick, N. J.: Rutgers University Press, 1951.

Frank, Lawrence K. The Conduct of Sex. New York: William Morrow, 1961.

Freud, Sigmund. A General Introduction to Psychoanalysis. Garden City, N. Y.: Garden City, 1920.

Freud, Sigmund. "The Sexual Enlightenment of Children," pp.36-44, Volume II, Collected Papers. London: Hogarth, 1924.

Freud, Sigmund. The Ego and the Id. London: Hogarth, 1927.

Freud, Sigmund. New Introductory Lectures on Psycho-analysis. New York: Norton, 1933.

Fromm, Erich. Man For Himself. New York: Rinehart, 1947.

Gagnon, John H. Human Sexualities. Glenview, Illinois: Scott, Foresman, 1977.

Goldstein, Bernard. Introduction to Human Sexuality. New York: McGraw-Hill, 1976.

Gorney, Roderic. The Human Agenda. New York: Simon & Schuster, 1972.

Greenwald, Harold. Direct Decision Therapy. San Diego: Edits, 1974.

Guttmacher, Alan F. "Who Owns Fertility: the Church, the State, or the Individual?", pp. 174-187, in Grummon, Donald L. & Barclay, Andrew M. (Editors) Sexuality: A Search for Perspective. New York: Van Nostrand Reinhold, 1971.

Guyon, Rene. The Ethics of Sexual Acts. New York: Knopf, 1948.

Guyon, Rene. Sexual Freedom. New York: Knopf, 1950.

Haire, Norman. "Introduction," in Bauer, Bernhard. Woman and Love. New York: Liveright, 1927.

Harper, Robert A. & Stokes, Walter. 45 Levels to Sexual Understanding and Enjoyment. Englewood Cliffs, N. J.: Prentice-Hall, 1971.

Harper, Robert A. "Moral Issues in Marital Counseling," pp. 48-57, in Ard, Ben N., Jr. & Ard, C. C. (Editors) Handbook of Marriage Counseling.

Hemming, James. Individual Morality. London: Panther Modern Society, 1970.

Henry, Jules. "The Social Function of child Sexuality in Pilaga Indian Culture," pp. 91-101, in Hoch, P. H. & Zubin, J. (Editors) Psychosexual Development in Health and Disease. New York: Grune & Stratton, 1949.

Hewetson, John. Sexual Freedom for the Young. London: Freedom Press, 1951.

Hiltner, Seward. Sex Ethics and the Kinsey Reports. New York: Association Press, 1953.

Holmes, Donald J. Psychotherapy. Boston: Little, Brown, 1972.

Horney, Karen. Neurosis and Human Growth. New York: Norton, 1950.

Hudson, John W. & Henze, Lura. "Campus Values in Mate Selection: a replication," pp. 73-79, in Wiseman, Jacqueline P. (Editor) People As Partners. San Francisco: Canfield Press, 1971.

Hunt, Morton. Sexual Behavior in the 1970's. Chicago: Playboy Press, 1974.

Huxley, T. H. & Huxley, Julian. Touchstone for Ethics. New York: Harper, 1947.

Johnson, Wendell. People in Quandries. New York: Harper, 1946.

Kaplan, Helen Singer. The New Sex Therapy. New York: Quadrangle, 1974.

Kardiner, Abram. "Orientation: Discussion," pp. 85-88, in Hoch, P. H. & zubin, J. (Editors) Psychosexual Development in Health and Disease. New York: Grune & Stratton, 1949.

Kardiner, Abram. Sex and Morality. New York: Bobbs-Merrill, 1954.

Kaufmann, Walter. Without Guilt and Justice. New York: Wyden, 1973.

Kekes, John. A Justification of Rationality. Albany: State University of New York Press, 1976.

Kinsey, A. C., et al. Sexual Behavior in the Human Male. Philadelphia: Saunders, 1948.

Kinsey, A. C., et al. Sexual Behavior in the Human Female. Philadelphia: Saunders, 1953.

Kirkendall, Lester A. Sex Education as Human Relations. New York: Inor,

1950.

Kirkendall, Lester A. Premarital Intercourse and Interpersonal Relationships. New York: Julian Press, 1961.

Kirkendall, Lester A. "Sex and Human Wholeness," pp. 278-290, in Grummon, Donald L. & Barclay, Andrew M. (Editors) Sexuality: A Search for Perspective. New York: Van Nostrand Reinhold, 1971.

Kirkendall, Lester A. "Sex and Social Policy," pp. 385-406, in Wiseman, Jacqueline (Editor) The Social Psychology of Sex. New York: Harper & Row, 1976.

Kirkendall, Lester A. "A Counselor Looks at Contraceptives for the Unmarried," pp. 303-317, in Ard, Ben N., Jr. & Ard, C. C. (Editors) Handbook of Marriage Counseling. Palo Alto: Science & Behavior Books, 2nd edition, 1976.

Langdon-Davies, John. Sex, Sin and Sanctity. London: Gollancz, 1954.

Lerner, Max. America as a Civilization. New York: Simon & Schuster, 1957.

Leuba, Clarence. Ethics in Sex Conduct. New York: Association Press, 1948.

London, Perry. "The Intimacy Gap," Psychology Today, Vol. 11, No. 12, pp. 40, 42-45, May 1978.

Mangasarian, M. M. The Bible Unveiled. Chicago: Independent Religious Society, Rationalist, 1911.

Margolis, Joseph. "The Question of Homosexuality," pp. 288-302, in Baker, Robert & Elliston, Frederick (Editors) Philosophy & Sex. Buffalo: Prometheus Books, 1975.

Maslow, A. H. "Self-actualizing People: A Study in Psychological Health," pp. 11-34, in Wolff, Werner (Editor) Personality: Symposium No. 1: Values in Personality Research. New York: Grune & Stratton, 1950.

Maslow, A. H. "Love in Healthy People," pp. 57-93, in Montague, Ashley (Editor) The Meaning of Love. New York: Julian, 1953.

Maslow, A. H. (Editor) New Knowledge in Human Values. New York: Harper, 1959.

Maslow, A. H. Toward a Psychology of Being. Princeton, N. J.: Van Nostrand, 2nd edition, 1968.

Masserman, Jules H. (Editor) Psychoanalysis and Human Values. New York: Grune & Stratton, 1960.

Masters, William H. & Johnson, Virginia E. Human Sexual Response. Boston; Little, Brown, 1966.

Masters, William H. & Johnson, Virginia E. Human Sexual Inadequacy. Boston: Little, Brown, 1970.

Masters, William H.; Johnson, Virginia E.; Kolodny, Robert C. (Editors) Ethical Issues in Sex Therapy and Research. Boston: Little, Brown, 1977.

May, Geoffrey. Social Control of Sex Expression. New York: Morrow, 1931.

Mead, Margaret. "Anthropology," pp. 53-74, in Wile, Ira S. (Editor) The Sex Life of the Unmarried Adult. New York: Vanguard Press, 1934.

Mead, Margaret. And Keep Your Powder Dry. New York: Morrow, 1942

Menninger, Karl. Whatever Became of Sin? New York, Hawthorn, 1973.

Meyer, Jon K. (Editor) Clinical Management of Sexual Disorders. Baltimore: Williams & Wilkins, 1976.

Morain, Lloyd & Morain, Mary. Humanism as the Next Step. Boston: Beacon Press, 1954.

Mowrer, O. Hobart. "Science, Sex and Values," Personnel and Guidance Journal, April, 1964, 745-753.

Murdock, George Peter. "The Social Regulation of Sexual Behavior," pp. 256-

266, in Hock, P. H. & Zubin, J. (Editors) <u>Psychosexual Development in Health and Disease</u>. New York: Grune & Stratton, 1949.

McCary, J. L. <u>Human Sexuality</u>. New York: Van Nostrand Reinhold, 2nd edition, 1973.

Nagel, Thomas. "Sexual Perversion," pp. 247-260, in Baker, Robert & Elliston, Frederick (Editors) <u>Philosophy & Sex</u>. Buffalo: Prometheus Books, 1975.

Newton-Smith, W. H. <u>The Rationality of Science</u>. London: Kegan Paul, 1981.

Otto, Max C. <u>Science and the Moral Life</u>. New York: New American Library, 1949.

Overing, Joanna (Editor) <u>Reason and Morality</u>. London: Tavistock, 1985.

Pittenger, W. Norman. <u>The Christian View of Sexual Behavior</u>. Greenwich, Conn.: Seabury Press, 1954.

Ploscowe, Morris. <u>Sex and the Law</u>. New York: Prentice-Hall, 1951.

Pomeroy, Wardell B. <u>Boys and Sex</u>. New York: Delacorte Press, 1968.

Pomeroy, Wardell B. <u>Girls and Sex</u>. New York: Delacorte Press, 1969.

Post, Seymour C. (Editor) <u>Moral Values and the Superego Concept</u>. New

214

York: International Universities Press, 1972.

Pruette, Lorine. "Conditions Today," pp. 278-303, in Wile, Ira S. (Editor) The Sex Life of the Unmarried Adult. New York: Vanguard Press, 1934.

Rapoport, Anatol. Science and the Goals of Man. New York: Harper, 1950.

Rapoport, Anatol. Operational Philosophy. New York: Harper, 1953.

Reichenbach, Hans. The Rise of Scientific Philosophy. Berkeley: University of California Press, 1951.

Reiss, Ira L. Premarital Sexual Standards in America. Glencoe: Illinois: Free Press, 1960.

Reiss, Ira L. The Social Context of Premarital Sexual Permissiveness. New York: Holt, Rinehart & Winston, 1967.

Robertson, J. M. A Short History of Morals. London: Watts, 1920.

Russell, Bertrand. Marriage and Morals. London: Unwin, 1929.

Schmalhausen, Samuel D. "Family Life: A Study in Pathology," pp. 275-303, in Calverton, V. F. & Schmalhausen, Samuel D. (Editors) The New Generation. New York: Macaulay, 1930.

Sears, Robert. <u>Survey of Objective Studies of Psychoanalytic Concepts</u>. New York: Social Science Research Council, 1947.

Seckel, Al (Editor) <u>Bertrand Russell on Ethics, Sex and Marriage</u>. Buffalo: Prometheus Books, 1987.

Slovenko, Ralph. <u>Psychiatry and Law</u>. Boston: Little, Brown, 1973.

Smith, Homer W. <u>Man and His Gods</u>. Boston: Little, Brown, 1952.

Socarides, Charles W. <u>Beyond Sexual Freedom</u>. New York: Quadrangle Books, 1975.

Stuart, Grace. <u>Conscience and Reason</u>. New York: Macmillan, 1951.

Taylor, Richard. <u>Having Love Affairs</u>. Buffalo: Prometheus Books, 1982.

Taylor, W. S. "A Critique of Sublimation in Males: A Study of Forty superior Single Men." <u>Genetic Psychology Monographs</u> 13:1-115; 1933.

Thompson, Clara. <u>Psychoanalysis: Evolution and Development</u>. New York: Hermitage House, 1950.

Vincent, Clark E. "The Cost of Naivete in Sex Education," pp. 15-23, in Farber, Seymour M. & Wilson, Roger H. L. (Editors) <u>Sex Education & the Teenager</u>. Berkeley: Diablo Press, 1967.

Waddington, C. H. The Scientific Attitude. New York: Penguin Books, 2nd edition, 1948.

White Amber Blanco. Ethics for Unbelievers. London: Routledge & Kegan Paul, 1948.

Wile, Ira S. (Editor) The Sex Life of the Unmarried Adult. New York: Vanguard Press, 1934.

Wolfe, Janet L. & Brand, Eileen (Editors) Twenty Years of Rational Therapy. New York: Institute for Rational Living, 1977.

Wylie, Philip. "Is Love Out of Season?" (A Review of Robert Elliot Fitch's book, The Decline and Fall of Sex) Saturday Review, August 3, 1957.

Young, Watland. Eros Denied. New York: Grove Press, 1964.

INDEX

DIMENSIONS OF ETHICAL THOUGHT

edited by Anthony E. Hartle and John Kekes

ISBN 0-8204-0590-6   300 pages   paperback US $ 21.00*

*Recommended price – alterations reserved

The book focuses on the nature of social and personal morality and on the relation between them. Each of its five parts begins with an introduction to a specific moral problem, presents a concrete case illustrating the problem, and then turns to a classical and a contemporary reading aiming to resolve the problem.

Its five parts are: The Common Good, Duties, Rights, Individuals and Society, and Happiness and Virtue. The book is an introductory text, suitable for a first course in ethics.

Anthony E. Hartle is an associate professor of philosophy at the United States Military Academy. He has combined academic and military careers, having taught at West Point for nine years while also serving in a wide variety of military assignments, ranging from commanding an infantry battalion to serving as a staff member on the Presidential Commission on the Space Shuttle *Challenger* Accident. Dr. Hartle, a colonel in the U.S. Army, has published in various philosophy and military journals.

John Kekes is Professor of Philosophy and Public Policy at the State University of New York at Albany. He is the author of *A Justification of Rationality* (1976), *The Nature of Philosophy* (1980), *The Examined Life* (1988), and over 60 scholarly articles on epistemology and ethics. He is a Rockefeller and an Earhart Fellow; the General Editor of a book series, *Studies in Moral Philosophy,* and a Consulting Editor of *History of Philosophy Quarterly* and *Public Affairs Quarterly.*

PETER LANG PUBLISHING, INC.
62 West 45th Street
USA – New York, NY 10036